Dedication

For My Husband Martin

Best wishes!
Gwen Petersen

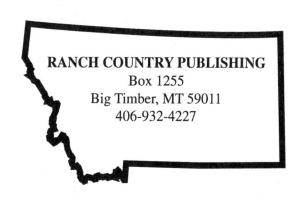

RANCH COUNTRY PUBLISHING
Box 1255
Big Timber, MT 59011
406-932-4227

Reprinted 1996

ISBN No. 0-943255-34-1

THE RANCH WOMAN'S MANUAL

by
Gwen Petersen

A handy guide and aid to those women choosing to spend their lives as RANCH WOMEN. Contains really helpful, practical, useful tips and hints to keep the Ranch Woman from going berserk.

Over the decades of rural living, Ranch Women have been helpmeets to their men. With remarkable courage, incredible stamina, and splendid insouciance to the rawer facts of nature, the Ranch Woman has shaped the nest surrounding that hard-workin', cow-wrasslin', bull-throwin' son-of-a-farmer.

Because farm and ranch life is necessarily divided and marked by the seasons of the year, The Manual will attempt to follow a similar pattern. Our hope is to provide an understanding reference volume (developed in secret women's conclaves*) (see footnote) for the dauntless ranch/farm wife, couched in language not necessarily comprehensible to men.

* Conclaves: referred to by ranch men as "gab-sessions".

THE RANCH WOMAN'S MANUAL

OUTLINE

by
Gwen Petersen

PART ONE: SPRINGTIME

SPRING: That time of year when the earth thaws and releases the frozen moisture, creating a thick dark gumbo usually tracked across the kitchen floor in artful patterns. The last of the hay for feeding the cows is running low and your man is worried for fear he'll be forced to buy more. He worries EVERY year.

Section One: Calving the Heifers

Wherein the ranch woman learns about the midnight duties required of a good Ranch Wife, and how to serve as midwife at the birth of a calf.

Section Two: Chickens

Wherein one learns about chicken manure, chicken house cleaning, egg gathering, setting hens, butchering roosters, chicken plucking and chick hatching.

Section Three: Pigs and Pigging

Wherein one learns that pigs require tender loving care and that it is the sympathetic Ranch Woman who can soothe a troubled sow. Pig care is considered a Womanly Art.

Section Four: Spring Farming and Crop Planting

Wherein one learns how to cope with mud, tired husbands and emergency breakdowns of equipment. One also learns instant weather appraisal and how to "talk weather".

Section Five: Starting the Irrigation Water

Wherein one learns that water must be managed and controlled. The good Ranch Woman learns to help tear out beaver dams, pick rocks, and ignore black moods of the damp ranch man.

Section Six: Hired Hands

Wherein one learns that the vagaries and varieties so richly dispersed among humans abound in hired men and/or couples.

Section Seven: Planting the Garden

Wherein one works like a fiend after coaxing husband (diplomatically) to plow. One plants rows and rows of potential foodstuff and resolves never to let one tiny miniscule weed mar the perfection.

Section Eight: Spreading and Harrowing

Wherein one learns that operating the manure spreader and harrowing the cowpiles are two ranch chores the ranch man ACTUALLY believes you're smart enough to do!

Section Nine: Instant Hired Hand

Wherein one learns how to become an instant expert at all ranch chores. One learns to accept second place to ranch critters having four legs and a tail.

Section Ten: Branding

Wherein one learns how to deal with tally sheets, vaccine guns and Mountain Oysters.

PART TWO: GOOD OLD SUMMERTIME

SUMMER: That time of year when one is impossibly busy,

the ranch bursts with life and company from the city descends in voracious hordes.

Section Eleven: Summer Irrigation

Wherein one learns what it is to cope with hired irrigators, husbands who work dawn til dark, and what potions and lotions to apply to cracked feet and blistered hands. One also learns about irrigating boots and how to reply to those dudes who want to know if you're goin' fishin'. And wherein one also learns how to hold the irrigating shovel.

Section Twelve: Haying

Wherein one learns to accept as normal, the preparation and serving of mountains of food to hay crews and how to haul a snack to the fields, plus complete advice on operating the tractor, the swather, the baler, and the mower, and make it appear that you know what you're doing.

Section Thirteen: Moving the Cows to Summer Pasture

Wherein one learns that you, as an incompetent instant hired hand, can lose a calf, but it takes an experienced cowman to lose a bull. One also receives lessons in correct vocabulary to employ while on a cattle drive, as well as the reason for starting the drive before dawn.

Section Fourteen: Veterinary Care

Wherein one learns how to haul a sick critter to the vet. One also learns what to do while a Veterinarian delivers a calf by Caesarean section.

Section Fifteen: Garden Maintenance

Wherein one learns to name weeds by their Anglo-Saxon sub-titles. One also learns the true aggressive nature of peas, beans and all garden vegetables. Advice is offered on how to Tom Sawyer the cucumbers.

Section Sixteen: Varmint Control

Wherein one learns that the beasts of nature are not on your side. One also learns how to get rid of magpies, coons, coyotes, foxes, and egg-sucking cats.

Section Seventeen: Summer Company

Wherein one learns that otherwise polite friends who live in the city, tend to look upon you, the Ranch Woman, as recreation leader for THEIR vacations. One learns some methods of ridding oneself of unwelcome visitors.

Section Eighteen: Canning, Freezing, and "Putting Up" All That Garden Produce

Wherein one learns that mother nature can overwhelm. One also learns that frontier life without electricity and freezers must have been hell.

Section Nineteen: Summer Fun

Wherein one learns the correct method of country tippling and how to dance country style.

PART THREE: FALL

FALL: A gorgeous and beautiful time of year when you can't believe summer is over. The critters grow lots of hair and a great deal of energy is spent discussing MARKET PRICES.

Section Twenty: Roundup Time and Marketing The Calves

Wherein one again becomes an instant cowpoke. One also learns that the stockyards are a man's world and after an hour, remarkably boring.

Section Twenty-one: Getting in the Wood for Winter

Wherein one learns how to operate the chain saw, throw

wood, stack wood, dump wood, and rick wood into neat piles. One also learns how to get the wood hauled from wood pile to stoves.

Section Twenty-two: Cleaning the Pig Sheds
(also done in spring)

Wherein one learns the important step-by-step method of efficacious shoveling of pig manure.

Section Twenty-three: The Art of Opening Gates

Wherein one learns how to open and close normal gates as well as husband gates.

Section Twenty-four: Hunting Season

Wherein one learns how to cope with those odd creatures— hunters. One learns what to tell them and what not to tell them. One also learns the correct method for helping husband butcher game meat.

PART FOUR: WINTER

WINTER: That time of year when one huddles a lot. Mornings are a misery if your sheepskin slippers have disappeared. And if the pipes have frozen in the night, that trip to the outhouse is pure agony.

Section Twenty-five: Feeding the Critters

Wherein one learns to drive the tractor or the pickup at snail's pace while your man throws bales to the cattle. One also learns how to throw the bales when husband throws his back out again.

Section Twenty-six: Proper Winter Clothing

Wherein one learns how the layered look is achieved for different temperatures.

Section Twenty-seven: Getting Ready for
Thanksgiving and Christmas Food Consumption

Wherein one learns to be grateful for all that stuff one canned and froze. One learns how to shortcut and come out smelling like a gourmet.

Section Twenty-eight: Surviving the Annual
Christmas Program at the Schoolhouse

Wherein one learns how to cope with the planned chaos of the annual school Christmas program.

Section Twenty-nine: Watching TV (if you have TV)

Wherein one learns that vast numbers of women wear makeup, fancy dresses, and high heels EVERY BLESSED DAY. And wherein you wonder how they would look wearing false eyelashes while feeding pigs in a blizzard.

Section Thirty: Waiting for Spring

Wherein one learns how to talk about the hard winter and how long the feed will hold out and what to do to avoid winter doldrums.

Section Thirty-one: Sheep and Lambing

Wherein one learns what to do as a ewe midwife.

PART FIVE: WOMAN WORK
AND WOMAN ACTIVITIES

"Woman Activity" includes all those community activities you do that you don't have time for but squeeze in anyhow. "Woman work" includes all those household duties and nasty maintenance chores, cleanup jobs, and eye-straining secretarial and bookkeeping tasks your man "lets" you do.

Section Thirty-two: Sleep

Wherein one learns that sleep is a forbidden luxury.

Section Thirty-three: Coffee and Cookies and Daily Meals

Wherein one learns that coffee and cookies are a country staple. One also learns country meal preparation and how to develop shortcuts for sanity's sake.

Section Thirty-four: Washing the Separator

Wherein one learns basic attitudes towards the milk separator.

Section Thirty-five: Visitors

Wherein one learns the proper rituals, customs and ettiquette when visiting or being visited. Wherein one also learns certain techniques to divest oneself of visitors while remaining polite.

Section Thirty-six: Coping with the Annual 4-H Fair

Wherein one learns how to bear up nobly.

Section Thirty-seven: Basic Ranch Attitudes

Wherein one learns that it only seems as though you take second place to the cattle, sheep and pigs. And wherein one knows that regardless of the overwhelming labor, the chapped and peeling complexion, the lack of "finer things", one still counts oneself the luckiest woman in the world.

PART ONE:

SPRINGTIME
ON THE RANCH

SPRING: That time of year when the earth thaws and releases the frozen moisture, creating a thick dark gumbo usually tracked across the kitchen floor in artful patterns. The last of the hay for feeding the cows is running low and your man is worried for fear he'll be forced to buy more. He worries EVERY year.

SECTION ONE: CALVING THE HEIFERS

Wherein the Ranch Woman learns about the midnight duties required of a good ranch wife, and how to play midwife at the birth of a calf.

When the two year old heifers are heavy with calf, your man makes many trips to the north pasture to check on possible new arrivals. Checking the heifers is an around-the-clock job in which you get to share. Your turn is the midnight and four a.m. tour. Bundle up to the eyebrows and arrange earmuffs.* (see footnote) Stuff your feet into your husband's old overshoes (for some reason one of your own boots has temporarily disappeared). Pick up the large flashlight with one mittened hand. Huddle deep into your muffler and track through the snow and the dark to the calving shed. Carefully check each and every heifer confined there. To check a heifer means shining your light on the delivery area for signs of an imminent grand opening. Usually the critters turn to stare at you staring at them. Then check each heifer just once more because you know you'll be chewed out if you miss one and she calves behind your back! Thankfully none of the girls seem ready to start yet. You pray they'll all wait for your husband.

Stagger back to the house and climb once more out of all those clothes. As you fall gratefully into bed, your man will cease snoring, open one eye and ask, "Everything all right?" Receiving an affirmative, he's instantly unconscious again.

However, not all your nighttime trips to the shed are so uneventful. More likely one of the darlings has begun the business of giving birth. Draw a deep breath and wonder what was so bad about secretarial work. Then inspect the situation. If the heifer is in labor, but nothing is poking out the back end, you're in luck. Tell the heifer to cross her legs, then as rapidly as mud or snow permits, stumble to the house where you awaken the cowman. What a relief to turn the problem over to him!

---

* Ranch men NEVER wear earmuffs. In fact, it has to be 20 below before they'll lower their earflaps.

Sometimes though, you'll discover a heifer down, moaning, and with two little feet protruding from her rear. She's in trouble. Resist the urge to panic and run for house and husband. Time is of the essence, he always more or less says. If the cow seems disinclined to get up, chances are she'll stay there while you work, you hope. Bravely shed your mittens, plunge your hands into the bucket of soapy water and disinfectant (you've kept this pushed down to the lid in the oat bin) and approach the young mother. Timing your efforts with the contractions, begin a steady pull on those two protruding legs. With any kind of luck you'll be strong enough to pop the little guy out of there. Recommended pull position is to sit spraddled on the floor, brace a foot on either haunch of mamma and pull like mad whenever she contracts. But sometimes nothing happens. Mamma is trying, you're trying, but the calf remains stuck. By now you're scared it'll suffocate. Should you race for the house and husband? Should you get the calf pullers? (A loop affair of chain on the end of a stick. You can slip the loop around the calf's legs up inside the mother and thereby achieve a much stouter grip and stronger pull.)

One thing you don't notice anymore is the cold. Your eyes are a little blurred though, from the tears of desperation. Rinsing your hands once again in the disinfectant, ease a hand into mamma. To your horror you discover it's a BREECH birth! Dear Lord, now you're sure the calf'll be dead when it finally arrives. Grab the calf pullers, slosh 'em in the disinfectant and ease the loop over those legs. Assume your spraddle-footed position. The heifer contracts mightily, you pull fiercely, teeth gritted and eyes squinted. You've just pleaded once again with the Almighty, when with a sudden slurpy release, the calf squishes forth. Whereupon you roll backwards into the fresh cowpile behind you. But clamber to your feet instantly, and hover over that calf. He's alive! Work his little legs back and forth and massage his sides. Finally, he lifts his head and blinks. By this time you're crooning a loving refrain to him as you hoist him up so you can iodine his navel.

Before you leave, make sure mamma is on her feet. Push the baby right under her nose so she'll get on with the job of licking him off.* (see footnote) Gather your tools, put away the bucket of disinfectant, find your mittens and stumble exhausted, but proud, for the house.

"Everything all right?" asks your loving man, as you wearily shed your smelly clothes.

"Just fine," you say. "That number 35 heifer had a nice big calf."

"Oh? Any trouble?"

"Well, a little," you say. "Mother and child doing well, but I DID have to . . . "

"Heifer or bull calf?" your beloved mumbles.

"A nice big bull calf," you respond warmly. "But he was backwards and I had to use the calf pullers and . . . " a wheezing snore interrupts your proud recital. Philosophically, you relax contentedly alongside the snorer, murmuring, "no— no trouble, dear, no trouble at all."

* Sometimes mamma is already on her feet and making menacing movements towards you. Do not stand there arguing about child care methods. Exit quickly.

SECTION TWO: CHICKENS

Wherein one learns about chicken manure, chicken house cleaning, egg gathering, setting hens, butchering roosters, chicken plucking and chick hatching.

Chickens are those remarkable feathered creatures that come in a variety of shapes, colors and sizes. But no matter how varied, once a chicken—always a chicken.

Generally, the man of the ranch or farm hates chickens. Probably due to chicken hysterics. A chicken is an inconsistent creature that squawks, flies up onto the shop roof, and nests in King-the-Collie's dog house. At egg gathering time, you must remember to check the dog house before King carries off the egg. Egg gathering is not exactly an art. Anyone can do it. Even number two son, age four and a half, can do it. However, gloves are recommended if you're chicken about sharp beaks. Occasionally you will meet a truly mean chicken. The treatment of choice is to plan stewed rooster for Sunday dinner. Especially if it's a large evil rooster inclined to attack defenseless small children, cats and dogs. In case of chicken attack when you are carrying eggs, hold the precious cargo aloft, leap high and karate kick with your foot at the fowl.

Number two son learns to develop a sharp eye and instant reflexes when dealing with the meanest rooster. Try not to scream, or panic when you glance out the kitchen window to observe Benny the Rooster sailing through the air, talons extended, to spike poor second son on his small behind, knocking him flat. With an ear-splitting scream, small son quickly hunches to his knees, scrambles to his feet and beats it for the house. All this he does with both fists doubled and held straight up over his head. The reason for this peculiar posture becomes apparent as he stalks into the house, hands still poked up over his head, marches to egg basket, carefully lowers his arms and deposits two eggs therein.

Frowning horribly, he about faces, stomps back out the door, pausing only to grab the broom. Benny the Rooster dodges for cover as a vengeful small boy tries to beat his brains out.

On the day you choose to butcher chickens, secure a short-handled axe, a sharp machete or a cleaver. * (see footnote) Keep the chicken house door closed (with chickens inside, of course). Slowly and quietly sneak in door. Then crouch and cover your head as thirty-seven hysterical chickens fly past and over. Grab one by the legs, ascertain that you wish it to be sacrificed, back out door and close it again. Fling the chicken on the block (hang on to the feet!), and grasp your decapitating tool in your other hand. A flung chicken automatically will extend its neck. Whereupon you guillotine it. Try not to think or imagine too much as the body runs and flops across the ground while the head lies there gasping and blinking. Simply go after another chicken.

When you've beheaded about six—quit. That's going to be enough plucking for anybody's day. Gather up the feathered bodies by the feet—three in each hand—and hold them out away from you so the blood doesn't spatter on your legs. Then run like mad for the plucking spot.

On the kitchen stove you've got a huge pot of water boiling. Drop chickens and fetch a pail of the hot water. Dunk one chicken at a time into water. Slosh it about for a few seconds. Then pull it out and start plucking. Pull feathers as fast as you can.** (see footnote)

Although you can pluck the big feathers from several chickens in just no time, it's those dinky pin feathers that ruin your record. Pin feathers are an important subject when discussing chicken plucking. It takes forever to get them all out. When you've achieved a pin-feather free fowl, it's time to singe your bird.

Chicken singeing is a must. The flame sears away chicken hairs left after plucking. Wad and twist newspaper, or squash and twist a paper sack. Strike a match to the end of your makeshift torch. Hold chicken and quickly pass the burning paper torch all over the bird. This method scorches off chicken hairs but is apt to scorch off your skin as well.

---

* If you can possibly secure your husband's services to wield the implement, do so. Or corral the neighbor, or anyone else available.

** Speedy chicken pluckers rate almost as high as home-baked bread artists.

Alternate method: A small flat tuna can half filled with alcohol, lacquer thinner, charcoal lighter fluid, or if desperate—gin, bourbon or brandy will flame nicely when touched with a match. This allows you to hold the chicken with both hands, thus insuring uniform singeing. CAUTION: If you use gin, bourbon or brandy, NEVER disclose this fact to your husband.

After singeing, you're ready to gut the bird. Take up your nice, freshly sharpened (by your dear husband) knife, and go at it your favorite way. (Actual gloppy details for gutting and cutting are described in the appendix.) After the birds are gutted, cut them up into the usual pieces, (unless you want to leave them whole for stewing or baking) and drop into a bucket of cold water to rinse. Remove, drain, and wrap 'em in butcher paper or drop in a plastic bag. Stick them all in that wonderful invention, the freezer.

If you feel there ought to be an easier way to reduce a chicken to the eating stage, there is. One way is to get someone else to butcher. Another is to skin the chicken rather than pluck the thing. However, your man will insist that the skin is the best part to eat!

At times it becomes necessary to CLEAN THE CHICKEN HOUSE of all that accumulated chicken guano.* (see footnote) A foul chore, but necessary only a few times a year. Pay no attention to those who do it more often. The tools of choice are the pitchfork, the grain shovel and a spade. What you do with these implements should be obvious. A wheelbarrow may be needed to transport the stuff. That treasure the chickens have been depositing for months must now be gathered up and re-deposited on your garden. Eventually you'll be through toting and carrying. Then kreosote the interior of the chicken house til you gasp for air. Put fresh straw in the laying boxes and on the floor. You are finished. You now resolve to allocate this chore to your oldest son since it is well known that shoveling chicken excrement is character building. Many politicians started out as common chicken shovelers.

* SMALL chicken houses are recommended. Shoveling chicken manure is easier if it's concentrated in a small area.

Hens are odd creatures. They yearn to become mothers. Anybody's egg will do. You'll discover hens in nooks and crannies all over the farm snuggled down tightly over their eggs, glaring balefully. There's something unnerving about the unblinking round-eyed stare of a setting hen. You can tell she's trying to set when she screeches wildly but won't LEAVE as you reach under for eggs. The peck holes on the back of your hand are some indication also.

Pay no attention to when the HENS want to set. Make them wait 'till spring so the little ones will have the warm summer to grow and prosper. Twenty-one days after you put a batch of FERTILE eggs under the hen, magic happens. Fuzzy little chirping creatures can be seen peeking from under mamma, who will fight to the death for her chicks. You've concientiously kept mamma fed and watered in her personal cage, checked the eggs a time or two, suffering peck wounds, but still you can't believe that's all there is to it! You just wish it had been that easy for you when your last son was born.

Keep mamma and chicks separated from the rest of the flock for a few days. When the chicks are strong enough, Mother Hen will parade the group out the door and into the pasture, clucking and scratching. The investigating house cat, sneaking too near, will receive a furious thrust from sharp talons. The smart cat needs only one lesson.

There are no absolutes when dealing with chickens. As an observant ranch wife, you will enjoy chicken antics and always name the roosters after your husband's friends.

SECTION THREE: PIGS AND PIGGING

Wherein one learns that pigs require tender loving care and that it is the sympathetic ranch woman who can soothe a troubled sow. Pig care is considered a Womanly Art.

Pigs are those fabled peculiar looking creatures credited with a variety of weird habits. Mostly the fables are exaggerations of the truth by frightened or uninformed persons. As with people, there are chauvinist pigs and there are fine swine.

The lord and master of the ranch or farm usually ignores pigs. He does not form attachments nor become emotionally involved. The Ranch Woman, on the other hand, can't think of anything cuter than a baby pig.

Grownup pigs will root through your fence and eat your garden. They'll root great holes in the irrigated pasture looking for angleworms. A pig will run amuck in the cornfield, chomping ears and tromping stalks. In fact, pigs force their way into or out of anywhere they want. It takes understanding to really love swine.

Pigs actually DO have "little piggy eyes" and "eat like hogs". Their manners are atrocious. The "boss" sow will steal food from the smaller pigs and they in turn chew out younger ones. There's no such thing as concern or fair play in the heart of a sow. Still, she's a friendly creature that loves to have you scratch her back, rub her stomach, or oil her itchy places. She'll come a-running when she hears you or sees you approaching. She'll hang around and talk to you when you are cleaning the sheds. She will also run over the top of you to get at a kernel of grain.

Some people read poetry about the "Children's Hour". You, as a Ranch Woman, can recite a good deal of blank verse about pigs. Your "swine song", as your husband puts it, includes admiration along with large doses of exasperation. When your favorite sow produces fourteen healthy babies, it's a fine feeling. When she mashes all of her 500 pounds on your instep, jams her huge head into the bucket you're carrying, almost separating your arm from the shoulder, a different sort of feeling pertains.

But the Ranch Woman has the touch with pigs. Women can talk pig. Communication on the deepest level exists between woman and sow. Betweeen man and pig, only suspicion and cold tolerance exist.

At pig feeding time (7:30 a.m. and 5:00 p.m.), you will cease whatever you're doing, and slip into your striped, one-piece ultra-charming coveralls. First, though, go to the bathroom, because a nature call while wearing the things can be awkward. Grab your gloves and don't forget your hat. Recommended hat styles are the baseball-cap type or the sailor hat style. These have enough brim to shade the eyes but not so much you'll keep knocking the blame thing off as you crawl in and out of pig pens.

As you start for the sheds, begin calling the pigs. There are several popular styles of pig calling. Choose one or make up your own. Pigs don't care. A favorite of the Ranch Woman is "come pig!" announced in a coaxing soprano. The ranch husband generally favors the deep-throated roar of no particular ennunciation, but immensely effective. Out of the brush will come galloping pigs, cattle, horses, and all flavors of farm animals. One feels sure elephants would also respond.

You commence to the sheds, pigs and dogs loping along in a loose caravan behind you. It is best to arm yourself with a stout stick when carrying the grain. The stick is employed as a deterrent to enthusiastic swine. Twelve 500-pound sows jostling you can lead to a loss of dignity. A sow attempting to dart between your legs is bound to be upsetting. Screams and threats on your part make no impression. But a stout clout on the snout with a stick will cause her to back away with an indignant squeal.

As you march rapidly from granary to feed stalls, wave the stick behind you giving the effect of a temporary tail. WARNING: Do not stop your forward progression! To pause is to be innundated by a dozen squealing sows, all of whom will try to dive into your grain bucket.

Each pig will choose her own feed stall, charge in, squeal, rear up on hind legs, and hang over the front edge of the stall, snorting and snuffling and generally raising an awful din. As you go down the row of stalls* (see footnote) dropping scoops of grain into troughs, a lovely peaceful quiet obtains, except for the unmannerly slurp-slurping. Lock the boss sow into her feed stall. Otherwise she gulps down her grain, scoots out backwards and tries to ram her way into the neighboring stall already filled with a sow. If the occupant doesn't instantly scramble out, the boss sow bites her on the rump, sending the poor thing into screeching hysterics.

As soon as the pigs finish their meal, they will beg and plead noisily for one more nibble of ration. But never listen to a seductive sow. If she gets too fat, she does not do well at farrowing time.** (see footnote)

Everything you've heard about "slopping the hogs" is true. In a bucket handy to the sink, save all table scraps, peelings, apple cores, onion skins, carrot tops—anything except coffee grounds and peach pits. Once a day, haul this goulash to the pigs. Or dump it into the separated milk your husband puts in the milk can out by the back door, and haul both milk and scraps at once. This divine mixture is called "slop" and the pigs adore it.

Farrowing time is an important event on the farm or ranch. In December and in June, the Lone Ranger (the boar) has done his duty by the girls. In spring and in fall, three months, three weeks, and three days after conception, it's time for the ladies' confinements. You've cleaned the pens in the farrowing shed (pig-shed cleaning is dealt with in another section), sprayed and disinfected everything in sight, strewn fresh oat straw in the farrowing beds and creep feeders.* (see footnote) Keep a watchful eye on the pregnant ladies and two or three days before the sow or gilt is due, shut her in her pen. You hope she will decide she likes her pen and wants to have her babies there. Caution: Don't wait too long to shut her up! A sow who decides to nest out in the timber can be highly resistive to alternate suggestions. That's if you can find her at all.

You have already prepared a medicine box containing clean

* The stalls are built in a long row—sort of like starting gates at a race track. An alleyway in front allows you to dish up the sows' dinners one by one.

** Farrowing: When the pregnant sows deliver their multiple blessed events.

* Creep feeder: a narrow space separated from the farrowing pen, equipped with heat lamp. Babies can get in and out but sows can't.

rags, scissors, iodine, alcohol and a magazine. The reading material is used to while away the time. Be sure it's light reading as concentration is difficult under a single hanging light bulb while sitting beside a farrowing sow.

It will usually be late when the sow pigs. One a.m. is a favorite hour. However, several hours before she lies down for her grand opening, a sow will "make her nest", which means she chews all the straw into little pieces, eats great chunks of wood from the sides of her pen, and several times, tries to climb out. She paces up and down in her pen, pausing to rip the trough off the wall where you thought you had it securely wired. Or else she grabs her food pan and flips it to the far side of the shed. It is not a good idea to be in the pen with her at this stage. She hurts, she's feverish, and she may inadvertently bite you in passing. But she doesn't mean it. When finally her pacing and chewing cease and her contractions begin, she will lie down quietly in her straw bed. That's when you climb into the pen with her, rub her tummy and tell her what a fine pig she is. After awhile, a contraction occurs and with a whoosh, out slips a little pig. From the second it hits the deck, it's on its own unless you're there. The new baby immediately begins to struggle and stagger from mamma's backend towards that long row of faucets. Mamma conveniently draws her top leg up and forward so junior can crawl over the bottom leg to reach his nourishment. Very quickly, the piglet drys off and begins on his life of eating. You, of course, have helped him by toweling him dry, and clipping and iodining his navel cord. For the next two to six hours, you will sit with mamma sow. In between the action, you read. Your thoughtful husband will bring you a thermos of coffee—sometimes spiked, and an egg sandwich on a paper plate. The egg will be runny, the fresh bread soft and crumbly and covered with a half inch of mayonnaise. However, you will feign gratefulness and eat the blobby thing, standing up in the farrowing pen, your hands scruffy and covered with iodine drizzle. At the first opportunity, try to toss some of the sandwich surreptiously into the next pen. Save the spiked coffee til last. If you are still in the pig parlor at mealtime, your dear husband will obligingly feed the offspring, and do up all the other chores except for washing the dishes or the separator, of course.

Finally the sow is finished. Ten or more lovely babies vie frantically for room at the lunch counter. Eventually each piglet will settle for one teat and will always come back to that same one.

Make sure the sow has plenty of water, clean up her afterbirth and spread fresh straw where needed. Deposit the little ones under the heat lamp in the creep a time or two. They'll usually crawl right back out to mamma, but from then on they'll return to the heat when cold.

Sometimes, the sow will have more babies than teats or a runt gets pushed off completely. Make sure the extra baby or the runt has swallowed a pretty good slug of that first colostrum milk from mamma. Then, as you leave the shed, pick up the little guy and stick him inside your shirt. He'll ride there while you drive back to the house where you fix up a lidded box-house for him. Put in a towel wrapped heat pad and some straw. Cut a "door" in one end. In a matching box, cut the whole end out, line with newspaper, and put in a heavy low sided dish of milk. The house box fits into the end of the milk box, giving a connected patio effect. The little pig, which by this time you've named "Portia", will snuggle down in her house and occasionally pop out for milk. The first night it's best if you hand feed her every couple of hours. Use a tablespoon and spoon in warmed cow's milk, or you can use a regular baby bottle if you wish. Some piglets take to a bottle instantly and others hate it. Within a day, the little piglet will be drinking nicely from her dish. Help her once or twice by stuffing her nose into the milk.

A baby pig makes a fine temporary pet. She'll adapt to anything. She likes to be scratched on her tummy and loves to be rocked. Unlike a human offspring, a baby pig will wiggle and squeal to get down when she wants to go potty.

SECTION FOUR: SPRING FARMING
AND CROP PLANTING

Wherein one learns how to cope with mud, tired husbands and emergency breakdowns of equipment. One also learns instant weather appraisal and how to "talk weather".

Spring farming and crop planting come at an inconvenient time of year—usually spring. Even if the calves are all on the ground, lambing is over, and the sows have all pigged, your husband is just not READY for planting. For several days now, the conversation has been about the weather. It is absolutely essential for the good ranch woman to learn to "talk weather".

In early spring, your man will cast an eye skyward, squint at the clouds and sniff. Sniffing is more prevalent in spring than at other times of the year. As he sniffs, he opines that spring is on its way and that a storm is in the air. He tests the ground for moisture and worries about wet weather and scoury calves. He tests the ground for lack of moisture and worries about drought. He observes snow clouds and worries about a spring blizzard and his meager supply of remaining hay. Your job is to nod in sympathy, cluck in agreement, and keep him fed and fit if possible. Because at that certain pause between good and bad weather conditions, your man will hit the crop-planting trail.

Suddenly the ground has thawed and awaits the plow, the fertilizer and the seed. Every year, the earth resists this intrusion. Mud puts out oozy tentacles that glom on to everything. For days your man has fretted that it's too wet to plow. He tinkers with machinery—oiling and bolting and sharpening. One morning, the dawn comes up smiling. So does your husband. Happily, he gulps his four eggs, six pancakes, hash browns, juice, coffee, and a quarter pound of bacon. Rising from the table, toothpick tilted rakishly, he claps hat on head, and strides out to meet the challenge of the tractor.

You watch as the tractor engine roars to life and away goes your knight on his tin horse.* (see footnote) An hour later, a

* All men are knights when driving a tractor.

totally demoralized husband returns to the house, spirit shattered. Drop everything instantly, pour coffee, and open the cookie jar. "What," you ask, "happened?"

Following a string of hair raising expletives, you learn: a) the tractor quit cold, or b) the tractor has a flat tire, or c) the plow broke entirely in half, or d) (and most likely) the tractor is hub deep in gluey mud and your man has spent the last half hour alternately digging, cursing, and kicking the defenseless machine.

If the problem is that the machinery has somehow broken, you are elected to "go to town for parts." You will be told to get a No. 273 dizzel for a 1969 tractor. In the meantime, husband will pill scoured calves* (see footnote) and put out some salt. He says that's why you have to go to town—he's too busy.

In town, the local garage is staffed with men of amazing perceptive powers who will know exactly what a No. 273 dizzel is. The garage men are always patronizingly kind. Patiently, they listen to your requests knowing you will inevitably have the wrong information. This time, though, you have carefully extracted a complete description and model number of the part needed from your husband. Confidently you smile at the parts man and announce your request. Your smile freezes as you hear that the dizzel comes in right or left, with or without a toggle. You pale—just like in stories. You haven't the faintest idea whether it's a right or left. You try to phone your husband. Naturally, he's out pilling the calves.

His last words were to hurry up—he's got to get that crop in before it rains again. Should you light out for home instantly? Or should you take four dizzels—two with, and two without toggles? Desperately you conjure up a picture of the tractor and your husband. Just which side of the tractor anatomy did he pull that dizzel from? It's no use. You can't telepathize the

* To pill a calf: First, catch animal. Then grasp him by his front legs and upend him so he appears to be sitting on your shoes, his back pressed against your legs. Reach in shirt pocket for scour pill. Stuff pill down throat of calf. Try not to let him bite fingers. Meanwhile, keep a sharp eye out for an irate mamma cow. Last: let him go.

Usually, you don't pill the calves, unless they are very tiny or very weak. Mostly your job is to follow along, shivering in the cold wind, and hand pills to husband as requested.

information. You tell the parts man you'll take all four dizzels and bring back what doesn't fit right away.

As you are about to hop back in the pickup, you notice you've got a great wad of some kind of sticky black substance all over your front. You deduce it came from the dizzel which you had carried warmly clutched to your person. The dark globs intermingled with the speckles of cherry juice (you had been constructing a cherry pie when the call for help came) make interesting, if tacky, designs. You feel, however, that these are proud emblems of the sacrifice you make for your beloved. That is, you feel that way til you are hailed by Mrs. Super Rancher. It's hard to hold on to your noble self-image when you turn to face her. She, of course, is clothed. You are barely dressed by comparison. Garbed in a reekingly elegant pants suit, she wants to know if you will bake some cookies for the church bazaar. Caught with no defense and totally intimidated by her warm super friendliness and that gorgeous outfit, you agree to create four dozen cookies for Tuesday. Which is tomorrow.

You and your box of dizzels escape into your mud splattered pickup. As you drive homeward, you have a semi-hysterical fit of giggling. Back at the ranch all is normal chaos. Your man is a picture of mud from futile efforts at extricating the tractor which he stuck in the mud right after you left.

Humbly you offer the box of dizzels, while framing your explanation for bringing back four of them. He doesn't listen. Happily he stirs around and pulls out one of the dizzels—without toggle.

"That's it!" he says. Then he picks up the box and stirs again, brow furrowed. With a sinking heart, you timidly ask what it is he's searching for.

"The flange! The flange! Where's the flange?"

You knew it. All along you really knew it had been far too simple a trip. It now appears you must return to town to get a No. 273 left hand dizzel without toggle, but WITH flange.

Keep a tight grip on your impulse to kill and comply without even changing out of your cherry-dizzel-grease outfit.

At nine o'clock that night, your exhausted man tells you how good the pie is as he finishes off his second piece—with ice cream. Your day-long mad dissipates. Reaching for a toothpick, he leans back in his chair. You prepare to listen closely to the account of plowing, planting, and getting stuck and unstuck.

SECTION FIVE: STARTING THE IRRIGATION WATER

Wherein one learns that water must be managed and controlled. The good Ranch Woman learns to help tear out beaver dams, pick rocks, and ignore black moods of the damp ranch man.

Irrigation Ditches: those peculiar snaky looking channels zigging through the hay meadows and circling the grain fields.

In spring, irrigation ditches on the ranch must be cleaned and water introduced into them. The main ditch, termed the "ragged assed ditch" by the local male wits, serves a large number of ranches. It travels for miles beginning where the river tumbles from the foothills of the mountains. Each spring, the ditch must be cleaned of the amazing amount of rocks, trees, twigs, leaves, and miscellaneous debris accumulated over the winter. Cleaning the Ditch becomes a community effort for the men. You will also share in the activity, never fear.

Each rancher on The Ditch has a certain number of inches of water he's allowed to take out.* (see footnote) Since irrigation water is the life blood of a ranch, an occasional difference of opinion can develop over just who gets how much water and when. Those ranchers located near the beginning of the main ditch tend to be calm friendly men able to view any situation with as objective eye. As the ditch proceeds towards the lower ranches, tension builds among otherwise friendly neighbors. The last man on the ditch spends a lot of his time cursing, jerking out neighboring headgates and insisting on his "rights".** (see footnote) The low man on the ditch is apt to develop serious personality problems. It's a lucky woman whose husband's ranch is on the upper end of the main ditch. She's even more fortunate if he's a dryland farmer.

Before Ditch Day actually arrives, several of the neighboring ranchers "stop by" to see your husband. You are prepared with a full cookie jar and plenty of coffee. Seated around the

* How those inches are measured remains a total mystery to all ranch women.
** Shovel-dented skulls are not uncommon among irrigators.

kitchen table, the men sidle into an agreement that TOMORROW IS THE DAY. The decision is reached during the last five minutes of the conference which has lasted for two hours.

As a loving helpmate, you do not hurry the conflab along. However, a private prayer is allowed, urging HIM to see fit to end the conference before 11:45 a.m. At that time, if the kitchen is still full of persons, country custom says you must invite ALL of them to stay for dinner. The conferees will look up, focussing upon you personally, for the first time that morning. All politely decline your invitation. But the first "no" doesn't count. You must eagerly repeat the invitation and elaborate by mentioning some part of the menu such as: "there's chocolate pie for dessert!" Again the guests will decline regretfully but with nostalgic comments about chocolate pie and congratulations to your husband (not to you) about what a good woman he has.

After the second refusal, it's reasonably safe to assume they'll all get up and leave shortly. The men initiate the leave-taking ritual by standing up, placing hats on heads and carrying used cups to the sink. They then bunch up by the kitchen door where the final arrangements for next day's program will be completed. It's quite possible your hospitable husband may still persuade one or two men to "stay for dinner".* (see footnote)

Early the next morning, a gaggle of men begin ditch cleaning. With backhoe and shovels, they will scoop out a wide assortment of debris that has accumulated over the winter. Ditch banks must be shored up and culverts cleaned.

As he leaves, your dear husband suggests that you start cleaning the lawn and garden ditches "if you've got the time." Long ago you somehow learned to avoid discussion of "time" and if you've got it or not. Therefore, after noon dinner, leave all the housework and go get ready to clean ditches.

Your ditch cleaning and irrigating costume are the same. Thigh-high, heavy rubber, ugly gray boots will chew your feet to a blistery pulp in no time. For some reason, it's not possible to buy boots other than too big. At each step, your foot comes

---

* Always be prepared for extra mouths with a backlog of eggs, bacon or sausage, and instant pudding.

up followed a half second later by the boot itself, making a shuffle-smack-thunk sound as you walk. Wear stout leather gloves which will get soaked, but will help prevent more serious wounds from the sharp sticks and heavy rocks. Caution: Do not use rubber gloves. They're slippery and you tend to drop hurtful stones on your toes.

In your jacket pocket, carry some chocolate bars.* (see footnote) At a casual angle over one shoulder, wear an irrigating shovel.** (see footnote). Over the other, a manure fork is balanced. Don't forget your hat—anything with a brim that doesn't fall off easily. Your pretty red and white speckled straw garden hat works well because it can be tied under the chin by its chiffon ribbon. You look a little like a chubby bent-elbowed, rubber-booted coolie.

Of course you know why you have been elected to clean the garden and lawn ditches. Its source of water is diverted from Antelope Creek rather than from the Main Ditch. And it's ALWAYS full of water. It wanders through the cottonwoods and meanders among the apple trees, across the nearest meadow and thence to your garden and lawn. Jump in at the garden end and begin scooping out sticks, twigs, leaves and rocks. The rocks tend to become heavier and heavier as you go. An hour and a half is the outside limit for stooping and lifting. So sit down for a chocolate bar break. As you try to get up to return to work you note you've acquired a semi-permanent forward-leaning posture. Still, maintain a cheerful attitude about it all. It's a lovely day. Except for the pain in your back, it's great to be outdoors. You're nearly through—just the half acre through the cottonwoods to go. You talk yourself into a rather sickening self-congratulatory Pollyanna attitude when you run into the beaver dam. The dam consists of a solid mass of interwoven sticks, twigs, leaves and small logs which have got to come out. A beaver dam is several feet long and wide and thick and you must unthread all those interlaced sticks, twigs, logs and slimy moss like a game of jackstraws. Always

---

* Chocolate bars are a must on most excursions. They can be used as an excuse to "take five" when you've reached the limit of endurance, and will fend off convulsions from hunger pangs.

** Irrigating shovel: a remarkable tool, sharpened on its business edge. It is used to shovel, chop, scoop, pound, mash and lean on.

you manage to yank on a key twig, pulling a hunk of the structure loose with a whoosh that sloshes icy water over the top of your boots. Your cold clammy feet now weigh a ton each. Go right ahead with your choice of curses and screams. No one will hear you and the extra emotion will help keep you warm.

With commendable bravery, you keep at it. Finally the ditch is clean, except for that one small boulder you simply couldn't budge. It's past chore time as you slish-slosh home, to find your loving husband has done the milking, the separating, and shut up the chickens. All you have to do is fix supper.

When your man announces he's been back for ages, and what's kept you so long, do nothing rash. Calmly and wordlessly remove your iron-rubber boots and wet socks. Pad into the bedroom and slip into HIS big wooley socks and HIS fleece-lined slippers. Then just as calmly, march on grateful feet back into the kitchen, reach into the lower left-hand cupboard and extract the large bottle of medicinal bourbon. Measure two generous toddies, sit down with your man and prepare to exchange ditch stories. Supper can wait.

SECTION SIX: HIRED HANDS

Wherein one learns that the vagaries and varieties so richly dispersed among humans, abound ten-fold in hired men and/or couples.

Spring brings variable weather, new calves, lambs, piglets— new beginnings of all kinds. For many ranches and farms, spring also brings hired men. If your operation is a one man, one family outfit, your husband likely needs extra help only in spring and summer. As **you** are always the instantly available hired hand, you think you will be glad to see a hired man come on the place. You've forgotten what happened last year.

Calving, lambing, pigging, cleaning the ditches, milking the cow, getting the wood up, barn cleaning, irrigation, spring planting and farming, fencing and haying are a few of the chores another hand could help with. Both you and your man are developing upset stomachs and short tempers trying to do all the additional work, attend all the spring functions at the school on behalf of your two sons and keep up with the usual time-consuming chores.

So one day your husband goes to town to "hire a man". The country hiring process effectively eliminates middle man services of an employment office. Your husband merely drops in at the Sheepherder's tavern, the Stockman's Bar, The Timber Inn, or the Longhorn Saloon. In each establishment he purchases a drink, hooks a foot over the rail, leans an elbow on the bar and commences discussing the weather, calves and spring planting with Sam the Bartender. Eventually the subject of hiring a hand slips casually into the conversation. Offhandedly your man will ask Sam if he knows of anyone looking for a job.* (see footnote)

Often Sam is able to produce a man for hire on the spot. It happens that at the other end of the bar, there leans a cowboy. He is drinking a short beer—slowly, striving for nonchalance.

"Here's a fella just said he was lookin'," says Sam. The job interview is then conducted on the spot, but first your husband

* All bartenders in male hangouts in a country town have been there forever and know everything.

orders another round of drinks. (The cowboy changes his order from beer to hard liquor.) As possible employer and potential employee negotiate, Sam and any other loose men standing around, interject helpful comments about the long hours, low pay, and horribly hard work to be endured if one is foolish enough to hire out to your husband.

If the first saloon stop does not yield a hired hand, your dauntless mate will try the next and the next and the next if necessary. Rarely can you expect him home before evening chores. The later his arrival, the cheerier his outlook—with or without a hired man.

The thinking Ranch Woman will have a thick stew and hot coffee ready the second he walks or lurches in. If your husband has had a successful trip, he will be followed through the door by the latest "hired hand".

Hired hands can be solid, faithful, hardworking men who devotedly care for the livestock and the land. However, more often a man is hired who demonstrates a definite personality quirk within the first day or two. His quirk usually interferes with his work.

As a Ranch Woman, you learn to categorize the transient help into types. There's the kind you think of as the "Slobberin' Joe" type. Slobberin' Joe never works anywhere longer than a month and a half. He derives his descriptive appellation from the fact that his constant chatter causes him to drool around his loose false teeth. He loves best to talk while chomping away on a giant stalk of celery, teeth clacking and moisture oozing from the corners of his mouth. Joe is also a butter-licker. After stabbing a hunk of butter from the dish, Slobberin' Joe juicily licks his knife and then stabs into the butter again for another gob.

If the new hand is not a Slobberin' Joe type, he may qualify as an "if only" sort. He is a man able and willing to tackle anything—he says. A heck of an irrigator—he says, "if only you had a sprinkler system." Often, he will relate at length how good he is with horses, "if only" he hadn't hurt his back when his last employer made him "lift those heavy bales." His tales of personal prowess go on and on.

You as a good Ranch Wife, are privileged to listen to If Only at the dinner table because naturally you get to cook for him as well. The If Only type is especially pleasant during meals. He considers it only courteous to include you in his endless commentaries, which means he compares anything you cook with the way his previous employer's wife (or cook) prepared the dish.

Fortunately, just as you are about to feed the man rhubarb leaf salad, he quits. But with a good excuse, of course. His back hurts him, his teeth need re-lining, he needs a haircut, his sinuses are acting up and his dear old Mother has passed on. He draws two months pay from your over generous husband, for his month and a half on the place, packs his gear and waits underfoot in your kitchen. While he waits for you to finish the dishes so you can drive him to town, he comments on your dishwashing style.

After "If Only's" departure, your husband hires another man who turns out to be a "watcher". A watcher, married or single, is usually quiet, soft-spoken, and terribly agreeable. His very quietness gives a misleading impression he can actually work. You will never know, since it's a rare moment that he turns his hand to any task if you or your husband are around to do it instead. On the day the Watcher is sent to the back pasture to get fence posts from the pile there, your mate has to go search for the fellow an hour later. The Watcher can't find the back pasture. Leading the way, your husband personally shows The Watcher the pasture and the posts. He (your husband) then loads them on the pickup while The Watcher watches. Occasionally the Watcher stoops to help lift the back end of a particularly long and awkward post. Or perhaps he'll let down the end gate of the vehicle to make it easier for your husband (or you) to slide the poles onto the pickup bed. The Watcher is semi-alert to any little thing he can see to do to make it easier for someone else to accomplish a chore. Often The Watcher combines watching with a persistent tuneless whistle.

Even though The Watcher watches such a lot, he suffers from dim vision and hearing loss, likely due to the constant whistling. Sent to check the ewes, The Watcher wanders right past a sheep bleating like mad and up to her neck in the slough. The Watcher reports all is well, but you can hear the commotion from inside the house. Respond to your uneasy feeling and go check the pasture yourself. Likely you will wind up alongside the ewe in the slough. Heave and shove her out, extricate yourself and take your soggy, gorpy self back to the house. As your drip up the path, The Watcher will hold open the backyard gate for your passage.

"Looks like you've been in the mud," he'll observe.

The Watcher is always prompt for meals. From a slow tender step that looks as though he's suffering from ring-bone, he swings into a smart canter when the dinner bell rings.

Very soon, you again haul the "hired man" to town, because your husband has fired him.

Next to follow The Watcher may be "The Decorators". Decorators always come in pairs. The man works on the ranch. The woman works anybody she can. Her aim is to extract as much as possible from the ranch owner. Always she begins her residency by redecorating the bunk house.

You personally have taken pains to keep the bunk house cottage freshly painted and repaired. Yellow curtains with white daisies blend with pine woodwork and cabinets in the kitchen. A stone fireplace in the living room complements the open beam ceiling. It's a cozy nest, furnished completely. But a Decorator is never satisfied. Usually she favors lavender and orangy-pink which she proceeds to calcimine all over the knotty-pine living room walls. Naturally she charges the paint to your account at the lumberyard.

After the Decorators leave, it requires considerable expenditure and time to have the woodwork and paneling electrically sanded and refinished.

Then there are the times your husband hires a wandering sheepherder usually named Sven or Olav or Sig. This type individual can drive you as an otherwise reasonably sane Ranch Woman into a nervous collapse. Sheepherder Sven is often mentally peculiar and downright crazy if he drinks. A Sven will talk to himself at length which doesn't bother you too much since you tend to do that yourself on occasion. But Sven argues with the voices in his head in his native language.

If Sven manages to imbibe too much liquor (his favorite pastime) he tends to become delusional and proceeds to disrobe entirely. Generally, that sort of display takes place in the town park where he then leaps faunlike among the pine trees. The town park is located across the street from the town grade school.

But when sober, Sven is a good hand with sheep. It is up to you and your husband to keep him pure, which means checking his clothing and his ancient pickup at frequent intervals for contraband booze. Eventually, the ranch loses Sven's services due to his untimely removal by the authorities to the local funny farm. One weekend, Sven went to town, got drunk and appeared stark naked at the coffee shop in the town hotel and a lot of people complained. Early morning streaking by a grizzled old sheepherder apparently depressed other patrons' appetites.

Sooner or later in the round of hired hands, Grammaw Charlie arrives. Grammaw Charlie paints. That's his one talent. He loves to paint. Hired to help with fencing and haying, his back goes out the second day on the place. So your husband puts him to painting the barn.

"Grammaw" earned his nickname due to his fussing habit. He's a champion fusser. He fusses about a spot of mud on the kitchen floor. He fusses about a mop until you fetch one for him. Then, fussing, he scrubs up the mud. He fusses because the mop is tattered and then he fusses because you didn't put down newspaper on his fresh cleaned floor. Charlie fusses with each stroke of paint applied to the barn. He fusses about the brushes, the color, the ladder, the paint thinner, and the hazards of inclement weather, such as a cloud, on his artwork. Your husband gets rid of Charlie by recommending him to a rancher at the other end of the county as a "good man with a paint brush."

Each hiring season, your ranch acquires a Tex or a Pecos or a Slim or some other colorful character. These men are always expert stockmen, they claim.

Last Chance Jones claimed he was the world's greatest hand with livestock. He favored a sparkly hat band on his huge black cowboy hat that complemented a black satin shirt with rhinestone buttons. Last Chance was a great rope twirler and fascinated both sons for two days. On the third day, however, the Sheriff drove into the yard and collected Last Chance. It seems the world's greatest roper and stockman was wanted for check artistry.

Odd personalities abound among hired hands, but since yours is a small outfit, you don't have near the problem your neighbor has. She contends with a whole wad of extra men and women all summer.

It's usually women who hire on as cooks. A good cook can be forgiven almost anything on a big outfit. Your neighboring ranch wife felt she'd tolerated enough when she found out the cook **charged** the men for mid-morning coffee and doughnuts. Your neighbor was puzzled as to why the men meekly paid up until she discovered the reason at three a.m. one morning. It seems the cook dispensed night-time favors to the men on a come as you are basis.

For some reason, women ranch cooks often have a history of selling personal favors commercially. Usually cheerful and easy going, such a lady will often advise you on her former occupation. Once while visiting your neighbor, her cook fascinated both of you with a detailed account of how to procure, what to charge, how to dress and what to say if questioned by nosey police. You and your neighbor took it all in. As good Ranch Women you should be open to educational experiences of all kinds.

Sometimes the ranch cook is an excellent chef, but prone to drunkenness and fits of temperament. The least upset causes the cook to reach for the bottle, whereupon, you, as instant substitute, have to fill in.

A drinking hired hand is unendingly exasperating. Often capable and alert (when sober), he quickly becomes useful and dependable on the ranch. You notice that the pressure of constantly running to keep up with the chores is beginning to ease. You are surprised when a whole month has gone by with no upsets or irritations. Then one day, right after payday, the hired man asks for a day off in the middle of the week. (It's also the middle of haying or some other major project.) He desperately needs, he says, a package of cigarettes, a haircut, a postage stamp, some new underwear, or a watchband. You feel an instant warning flutter in the pit of your stomach. You offer to bring him cigarettes and mention that you're a whiz at haircutting. No matter what you say, he has a flanking argument, including the passing of his dear old mother.

He goes cheerfully, promising to be back in time for supper.

Three days or more later, the phone will ring. It's Sam the Bartender inquiring if you want the man back or should he call the Sheriff. Your husband may take him back hoping to get another one-half month's work out of him before the next binge. Usually, it's your spouse who goes to town to collect the fellow. But sometimes, you, as the person-who-can-always-be counted-on, find yourself driving to town after a sick and broke cowboy. You've had experience before, so you know what to expect. Expectations are fulfilled. Sam, the bartender, has stashed Willie, the hired hand, in the Snake-pit.* (see footnote) Sam helps you lead him to the pickup. Meanwhile, Willie sings his version of "On Top of Old Smokey".

It's a warm day and Willie has neglected bathing recently, so crank the windows down. Sam straps him onto the seat with the seat belt. Between verses of his song, Willie pleads for "one more lil drink." You say absolutely nothing. Think of Willie as a difficult critter which has to be corraled and trucked home. Never try to talk, reason or plead with a drunk. Repeat: do not respond no matter what he says.

Back the pickup away from the curb and drive around the corner to the United States Post Office. Like a dope, you forgot to go to the Post Office first and pick up that package of vaccines. But you must chance it. Willie is strapped in, his song reduced to a dull rasp. Quickly hop out of pickup, scuttle into Post Office and pick up your package. You're breaking for the door when you are accosted by Mrs. Super Rancher. She wants to know if you're coming to the Club meeting tomorrow. Chat superficially, but try to hurry her along. You're terrified that Willie will escape and you'll have to give chase. You and Mrs. Super Rancher reach the sidewalk in front of the Post Office where your outfit is parked at an angle. At that moment Willie leans out the open window and vomits.

Feeling pretty nauseus yourself, turn to Mrs. Super Rancher and remark lightly "see you at Club." Quickly, dart around to the driver's side, pile in and back away from the curb. As you maneuver the vehicle into the driving lane, you catch Mrs.

* Snake-Pit: a small dark room with benches where drunks sleep it off or climb the walls according to their needs. Kindly Sam brings them coffee and soup til they're fit to stagger forth.

Super Rancher's eye. Flash a super charming smile, twinkle your fingers at her and gun the motor.

No matter how odd or peculiar the men may be, as a good Ranch Wife you must be prepared at all times to act as den mother to hired hands. You may "boss" a hired hand if you stick to orders regarding meal times or the cleaning of muddy boots. You can go so far as to "request" a load of wood to be carried in for the cookstove. But never, never order a hand to do any of the "real" ranch work.* (see footnote) Such directives are the prerogative of the ranch man only. It is sometimes OK to relay a message from your husband to the hired hand in extreme emergency.

If you, as a female, attempt to direct a hand to start fencing the lower pasture, for example, you will find the man has developed acute deafness. Recommendation: If you want the fencing (or any other task) started and your man isn't home to issue the order, there are alternate ways to approach the problem. First, obviously park the pickup in front of the shop door. Then fetch and carry fencing tools and wire to the vehicle. Load some poles and lastly throw in a sharpened spade. You have arranged it so the hired man notes all this activity. Mention to him you're going to the lower pasture to do some fencing and laughingly joke you hope you don't cut your hand open on the barbed wire "like last time." Give the hired man plenty of time to ask "if you'd like some help." To which you reply "do you have the time? I'd appreciate it. If you'll drive, I'll open the gates." Whereupon both of you commence to the lower pasture where you hold and hand things while the hired man stretches wire and pounds staples. When you become bored, mention you have to check on the bread rising and then walk home. If it's too far to walk, take the pickup and lie that you'll be right back. At home, wait for number one son to arrive from school and send him after the hired man. Number one son is twelve and loves an excuse to drive anywhere.

* The only time a woman may give orders is if her husband is sick, in the hospital or dead.

SECTION SEVEN: PLANTING THE GARDEN

Wherein one works like a fiend after coaxing husband (diplomatically) to plow. One plants rows and rows of potential foodstuff and resolves NEVER to let one tiny miniscule weed show itself.

Considering all the peculiarly titled country-western songs on the air, there should be one labeled "When It's Garden Planting Time, Smile and Let the Dishes Go Undone-Blues".

This year the garden shall be beautiful—your annual noble resolve. A garden is a major part of a Ranch Woman's spring, and especially summer, life. Lucky and blessed is the woman with a green thumb. For her, everything grows, the birds sing and eat only the slugs, and weeds are timid fragile growths of no importance. The neighbor's garden is one of those—a magazine picture of planned beauty and productiveness. Your own garden has a more utilitarian appearance. But this year you determine things will be different.

Stashed away in the cupboard behind the ice-cream freezer on the porch are $26.50 worth of seeds ordered from five different seed companies. The circus bright packets hold exciting varieties of vegetables, cucumbers, canteloupe, squash, four kinds of corn, pumpkins, peppers, and spices and herbs of all sorts. Plant these practical seeds in a large sunny plot beside the house. Along the walks and in front and back yard, go wild with a rich profusion of flowers and shrubs—all planned to bloom with glorious color all summer long.

This year you are determined to be efficient. Commence by drawing a Master Plan on paper. After the Master Plan, the next major hurdle is to prevail upon the Master of the House to implement your Master Plan by plowing the garden. For some reason, garden plowing is always last in your husband's mind.* (see footnote) First he must plow the oatfield. Then a spare part must be purchased before the tractor can function

---

* Investigation by a select committee of Ranch Women reveals that resistance to garden plowing stems from childhood. As boy children, the men were forced to weed, till, hoe, plant and water. Pay no attention to this, however. Force your sons as well.

again. Or he claims the ground is too wet, or there was a frost and the ground is too hard. Or the widow woman down the road has to have HER garden plowed. "She's alone," your man says. "It won't hurt to help her out."* (see footnote)

If gentle pleading at breakfast does not produce results, the thinking Ranch Woman must resort to other tactics. Have a headache when you retire because of "worry about putting the garden in." This works sometimes, especially if you've thoughtfully purchased a copy of Playboy and left it on your spouse's pillow. Next morning, bake an enormous chocolate fudge cake and smear on thick chocolate fudge frosting. Mix up some pink icing, decorate the cake edges with pink roses and in the middle, write:

Grand Prize

Garden Plowing

Do not serve 'til after plowing is actually finished.

After all the hard won plowing and fertilizing, the garden is left with big black curds which have to be tilled to manageable size. Then the soil must be raked level and smooth. Dig out your rubber gardening boots** (see footnote) which will be found under the stairs leading to the basement. Find some thinish leather or plastic garden gloves and don your striped bib overalls. The red speckled straw hat with the chiffon tie completes the ensemble. Stock your pockets with Kleenex because all the bending and stooping makes your nose run.

A runny nose is the least of the bodily disorders that occur as a result of gardening. When your back reaches an unbearable level of pain, be ready with certain remedies. First of all, try not to bend and stoop. Drop to hands and knees and crawl. The rows may become crooked, but pay no attention. Remedy two: At 4 p.m., after a brutal gardening session, go to house, draw a deep hot bath to immerse self for 30 full minutes. Do not start timing 'til you are in tub. Take with you some reading material that won't tax your mind too severely such as a mystery or a gothic novel. Remedy three: When it becomes

* You can't beat this particular excuse, so send along a jar of last year's mint jelly and a loaf of fresh homemade bread.

** Garden rubbers: either those old red rubber boots you wore years ago in high school, or cut-off irrigating boots that developed leaks, making them unfit for ditch work.

apparent you are crippled beyond a home remedy's capacity to cure, go see the chiropractor. He will push, pull and wiggle your warped spine back into alignment. In addition, your disability will then achieve the status of needing medical attention.

Direct orders accompanied by awful threats encourage both sons to help with the backbreaking labor. Finally, the lovely, thick, black velvet carpet of earth looks up at you. Whip out the Master Plan and the seeds. If you are one of the fortunate green-thumb Ranch Women, you know exactly what to do. Automatically, the spacing, the depth, the loaminess, or non-loaminess of the soil, and the proper sequence of the planting fall into place. You, however, consult the directions on the backs of the seed packets. Rake, dredge, poke, hoe, pat and tromp. After awhile you will have impregnated the black earth with thirty-four semi-straight rows of seeds. The garden fairly hums with life.

Faithful garden watering is a must. Assign watering chores to the offspring which helps teach them the lure and lore of growing things.

Put in heaps of potatoes, onions, corn and green vegetables. Hardy seeds can be planted outdoors early in the spring. Those seeds started in the house require a different approach. Gather peat pots, paper cartons, styrofoam cups and odd shaped plastic cheese dip containers. In these, plant herbs, spices, flowers and especially tomatoes. Such plants must be started in the house in order to reach enough maturity to be transplanted outdoors.

Start the tomato seeds in individual earth-filled peat pots and set the pots (at least twenty) in your extra large baking pan or in old refrigerator trays. Since all the southwest windows and ledges are overflowing with potted things, the tomato plant trays live with you in the kitchen. One tray filled with little thready green plants decorates the kitchen table edge next to the window. Eating is still possible, if crowded. Keep a vigilant eye on Blossom, the housecat. It is best to leave a special eight-inch space in the sunniest window for Blossom to sit. Otherwise she deliberately paws to the floor each tender potted plant. Firmly discourage her from eating the fresh green shoots. Smacking her with a fly swatter is usually effective.

Successful tomato raising is a matter of pride to the Ranch Woman. Once transplanted in the ground, protect the little dears from high winds and possible unexpected late frost. Stick some of those old left over shingles around each plant at all four points of the compass. If you're out of shingles, look out behind the old well house and swipe some of the worn cut tires your husband has been saving. These make excellent protective wind breaks. Til all possible danger of frost is past, each and every night, cover the plants with old sheets, gunny sacks, old dam canvass, or old tablecloths. Each and every morning remove them. Almost always, you forget to cover the plants til you're ready for bed, and can't find your slippers. With true Ranch Woman resourcefulness, slip into your husband's footgear and his big warm bathrobe. Find the flashlight, scuff into the garden, and flop the coverings over the plants. Ignore the fact that the hem of your husband's robe is becoming soggy and think only what a truly conscientious person you are. Remember, frozen tomato plants are one of the worst tragedies that can occur in a gardening career.

As a true blue gardening Ranch Woman or merely one with good intentions, you must construct a compost heap. In a corner of the garden reserve an area about two kitchen tables in size. Gather grass clippings, old bedding straw from the pig shed, all the leaves raked from the yard in the fall, vegetable peelings and some of the free sawdust you got from the sawmill and pile in alternating layers with manure. Any kind of manure will do, although chicken and sheep are considered to have the greatest fertilizing power. They certainly smell that way. Make the manure layers thin, and the leaves and other material six to eight inches thick. Some scientific super gardeners will put their compost in a giant box with hinged lid. When all inside deteriorates and rots through and through, super gardeners spoon out the stuff in measured amounts onto the soil. Pay no attention to all that. Remember the Ranch Woman's simple directive: "Pile it up, let it rot, and put it on." However, you needn't bandy your methods to anyone. When the compost heap enters the conversation, always sound completely knowledgeable by discussing in positive tones, each layer of rotten stuff, its depth, its consistency, and its potency.

SECTION EIGHT: SPREADING AND HARROWING

Wherein one learns that operating the manure spreader and harrowing the cowpiles are two ranch chores the ranch man ACTUALLY believes you're smart enough to do.

Ranching and farming are occupations constantly concerned with animal manure. Its collection and dispersal are important springtime duties. "Money-in-the-bank" is an oft-repeated slogan.

Throughout the winter, from the cow barn, the pig shed, the chicken house and the sheep shed, the stuff has been regularly scooped up and tossed onto an ever growing pile. The cow barn even has a special window out of which to pitch manure. By spring, the heap reaches as high as the windowsill. The roosters enjoy climbing to the peak of manure for a good crow and pigs will scale the summit to jump through the open window into the barn to steal grain. The piles down by the pig sheds and the sheep shed have also reached impressive dimensions. All winter you've been wheel-barrowing the stuff onto the heaps. It is now time to utilize all this home manufactured fertilizer.

To the tune of terrifically clever remarks, your husband and number one son fill the manure spreader one shovelful at a time. If you're lucky enough to have a front loader for the tractor, the job can be accomplished in no time. Number one son will miss a meal just to get to scoop manure.

A manure spreader is a long, usually green, box affair on wheels. Situated at the back end of the thing is a great large spiked horizontal cylinder thing that looks like a huge bristled hair curler. Somehow this whole contraption turns when the spreader is hitched to the tractor.

Try to arrange it so your husband will "let" you drive the manure spreader even if you have to hitch up the loaded spreader yourself.* (see footnote)

Begin at the lower corner of the hay meadow and line out the tractor with the manure spreader following faithfully behind.

* As a good Ranch Woman you learn to hitch up and operate all the farm equipment. WARNING: Take Care! All ranch machinery is stealthily hostile to women and will pinch, bruise and bash.

Reach down, pull that short handled knob to half position and commence spreading. Which means that as the hair curler turns on a steel track arrangement, the heaped manure is combed off the end of the spreader. The manure doesn't merely drop quietly to the ground, though. With joyful abandon, small flakes and globules of the stuff fly up and up into the air to rain back to earth. Most of the material flies straight up and you've driven ahead before it has a chance to fall back on you. But there are always occasional flying curds that seek you out, especially if you've just washed your hair.* (see footnote) A wide brim straw hat, leather driving gloves, overalls and denim jacket is the ensemble of choice for this operation. Somehow the combination of fresh sunny air, the buzz of the tractor and the excitement of the flying fertilizer arouses your urge to sing. Hymns and spirituals lend themselves particularly well, so as you sweep around the meadow, let go with a hearty, "Ro-o-c-k of A-a-a-ges-s-s."

Through the winter, the cattle have been pastured and fed on some of the hay meadows. Cattle are roving creatures and have done a good job depositing their droppings at random all over the fields. Before the spring thaw, feeding the cattle demands skill, a sturdy vehicle and a sound body. Both body and vehicle must withstand the spine cracking, teeth rattling, jarring and thumping which occurs as you bounce over terrain littered with frozen cow pies. In winter, a fresh dropped cow pie turns to instant cement which miraculously softens as the weather warms. The problem now becomes one of dispersion. A cow pie that just sits there in its own juices eventually dries to a pancake which smothers the grass under it. So one fine warm spring day your man will ask, "Do you have time to harrow?"* (see footnote)

Harrows come in a variety of styles. A favorite instrument is that contraption of steel, grill-like arrangements alternating with hard wood poles. The whole looks like jail house barred windows laid flat on the ground and linked together by a system of chains.** (see footnote)

* If the wind is blowing, reconsider spreading for that day.
* As a good Ranch Woman, you always have time for a harrowing experience.
** Harrows can be home built out of random pieces of iron pipe, wagon spokes, old tires, and old hot water radiators. Ranch men have been known to spend whole days happily knitting all this together.

Garb yourself in denim jacket, grab your straw hat and wear leather gloves. No special requirements for coveralls or overalls. Regular jeans and natural cushioning will do. Mount the tractor steed and charge the field. (Your thoughtful husband has hitched the harrow to the tractor for you.) Begin at the fence corner and drive over the field in ever diminishing circles. The harrow bounces along behind, crashing into the cow piles, mashing and mauling them into acceptable sprinkles of manure. While harrowing, the Ranch Woman is completely free of the house for a time. As you watch the harrow chew away at the cow pies, the sun warms your back, and a beautiful peaceful chunk of time happens to you. Sometimes you think you'd like to write a book—if you ever get time.

SECTION NINE: HELPING OUT ON THE RANCH OR; INSTANT HIRED HAND

Wherein one learns how to become an instant expert at all ranch chores. One learns to accept second place to any ranch critters having four legs and a tail.

The Ranch Husband sometimes needs his woman to drive the tractor while he feeds the cattle, or vaccinate the calves while he holds 'em, or hold 'em while he castrates 'em and brands 'em. In any case, you must be an instant expert in all phases. You will learn to employ muscles not normally used by women or even elephants. If you're really good, you may earn that best of all songs of praise, "she's a hell-of-a-hand!"

Try very hard not to take personally the adjectives coloring the air, especially when working with the stock. A poor innocent cow, sheep, or pig takes on amazing qualities and spurious ancestry when husband is discussing them in the corrals and through the chutes.

Of equal importance are the following commandments for an I.H.H.* (see footnote) woman.

1. Keep mouth shut and body alert and poised to jump in all directions.

2. Be brave, selectively deaf, and keep mouth shut when the language becomes more and more virulent.

3. NEVER try to lighten the situation with pleasantries or observations on the beauty of the day.

4. NEVER, NEVER point out an error or goof or alternate method of approaching the task.

5. NEVER, NEVER, NEVER giggle at the cute antics of the animals while your man is physically engaged in working with them.

Even when observing the commandments, some days are unbearable. If, in spite of every precaution taken, the situation begins to deteriorate into an emotional catastrophe, there is only one thing left to do. Put down whatever implement you're holding and begin quietly to cry. Turn on your heel and go to the house. This action MUST be carried out without speaking

* I.H.H.: Instant Hired Hand

a word and without looking back. Earplugs at this point, are of particular value.

Your duties as an Instant Hired Hand occur on an emergency basis always. Your man saddles up to bring in cows from the South 40. As he rides past the kitchen window, he bellows for you to come watch the gates. Scrape the bread dough off your hands, grab your wide-brim hat and don't forget gloves. (Gates have a tendency to impale you with splinters.) Gallop on foot for the corrals.

Across the lower meadows, you observe a thundering herd of cows and calves blasting towards the big pole corral gate. That's the very same gate you are prepared to swing open, then duck out of the way so you don't spook the critters. With flourish* (see footnote), you shoulder open the heavy pole gate and wrestle it to wide open position. All goes well. The cows rip into the corral and begin to mill around. You slip to the gate to close it. (All gates are harder to close than to open.) Try not to panic as you keep an eye peeled for that mean, wild-eyed roan. With the gate half way shut, the roan roars out an awful bellow and gallops towards the slowly closing aperture. As you stare in horror at the charging cow, you're also aware that your man and the REGULAR hired hand are riding up fast. As a good Ranch Woman, you will die before you let that darn cow escape through that gate! From depths you are surprised you possess, emit a horrifying howl. Leap two feet up and three over to land in front of the charging critter. Sweep your hat off your head and wham it in wide smashing arcs before you. If you can stand it, keep your eyes open so you can tell if your actions are effective. At this point, you will discover brand new Anglo-Saxon names for Bossie. But you win. The old cow circles away and back to the herd. Proudly finish closing the gate and assume your best air-of-nonchalance.* (see footnote) Maintain your air as your grinning husband swings off his horse to observe, "that old slut is wilder than a peach orchard boar!" Take it for granted he means the cow.

Probably the least exciting I.H.H. duty is the thing-holding chore. Your man, especially on a rainy day, asks you to come

* To achieve gate opening flourish, pretend you are a star football tackler hitting the line.

* Ranch Women are masters of the Art of Assumed Nonchalance.

help him in the shop for a minute. That means you will spend a slow age handing him nails, nuts, bolts and assorted tools. Mainly, however, you hold things such as one end of an iron thing while husband operates on the other. Or steadying boards while he saws or handing up shingles while he nails. You can't sit down, you can't leave and grunts are the only response to attempted conversation. Caution: Do not make the mistake of assuming an INTEREST in what your man is doing. Inevitably, this leads to comment and helpful advice from you which is bound to be rejected—probably nastily. Try instead, to invent new recipes in your head using weird combinations of ingredients. Serve it for supper as a shop-worn special.

Sometimes you are called upon "just for a minute" to ride along while your man "brings in that cow with the foot rot." For some reason, this always develops into a triangle. One point of the triangle is your man—driving the pickup slowly in the wake of the limping cow. Another point is the cow, ambling down the road with an occasional glance from side to side. The third point of the triangle is you—on foot—jog trotting along at the proper distance to keep the cow's mind pointed forward towards the corrals. Your job is to sprint like mad to cries (from the pickup) of, "head 'er off! head 'er off!!" when she tries to duck back. Then, at the precise moment, learned only through experience, you lope quickly ahead, swing open the gate, and gallop back to position. Your man, meanwhile, has been banging the sides of the pickup to promote continued forward movement of the critter. After cow and pickup have passed through the gate, close it. Then you may ride the rest of the way.

Sometimes you are privileged to help doctor a cow in the open without benefit of corrals or chute, especially on Sunday, the hired man's day off. Your man claims he's got to vaccinate "that number 35 heifer." You are requested to go along to "hold the vaccine gun." "She's in the small pasture down by the creek and she's gentle," your man claims.* (see footnote) "I'll just rope her and snub her to a tree." He further adds your only duty will be to hand him the vaccine gun at the proper moment.

* Any critter not actually a killer is termed "gentle".

Well, what else can you do? As a good Ranch Woman, you smile and make ready for a fun outing. Don't forget your hat and your leather gloves.

Admiringly, you watch as your stalwart husband quietly slips up on the chosen heifer and skillfully eases the loop over her horns. With an expert wrench he ducks around a sapling, wrapping his end of the rope around it. At the other end of the lariet, that "gentle" heifer is going crazy—jerking, pulling, snorting and bawling. Somehow, your man doesn't seem to see or hear anything. "Hand me the vaccine gun," he requests, leaning hard on his end of the rope. You hand him. "Here," he says, "hold this." You exchange vaccine gun for the rope! "Keep it tight," says your man. (Don't bother to wonder why he thinks you wouldn't.) Recommended stance for holding lariet rope while critter occupies other end: Pass rope behind you as though you're going to sit on it. This allows you to use all that ample posterior muscle as added leverage. So there you are, hanging on to a rope that has a captured, argumentative cow at its other end. Offer prayerful thanks for the wrap on the sapling. For a few seconds the scene is a frozen pastoral tableau. The heifer faces you, head down, pulling mightily against the rope. If she'll hold that position, your man can slip up and stick her before she knows it. As your husband poises his needle, the heifer does a ballet leap straight up and comes down charging straight at you. "Hold her! Hold her!" instructs your man. (You couldn't possibly NOT hold because you're too terror stricken to let go.) The cow hits the end of her tether at the sapling. You are saved. Then she sunfishes around and begins to circle the sapling UNWINDING that wrapped rope! Now is the auspicious time to move. Still hanging onto the lariet, zoom around the sapling rewinding the rope faster than the heifer unwinds it. Fortunately, just as you are seriously considering abandoning the whole project, the critter plants her feet and hauls back on the rope. Immediately assume your semi-seated stance on the taut rope.

"Got her?" asks your man. You are safe in assuming this to be a rhetorical question. This time your husband succeeds in jabbing the heifer in her hip. She doesn't even move, only stares hatefully at you. Your man relieves you of your end of the lariet, frees the heifer, who trots five feet away and begins to graze, totally unconcerned.

"There, that wasn't bad," states your dearly beloved. Assume your best air-of-nonchalance and agree.

SECTION TEN: BRANDING

Wherein one learns how to deal with tally sheets, vaccine guns and Mountain Oysters.

On branding day (the day when your ranch mark is burned into the hides of all those fresh-faced baby calves) you do double duty. Not only do you act as hired hand, but you're also chief cook, hostess and runner-after of anything anybody has forgotten. Sometimes a day of indescribable hilarity, sometimes laced with small tragedies, branding is always a whole lot of work. As a thinking Ranch Wife, estimate how many neighbors and extra hands are coming to "help", add fifteen, and lay in mountains of provisions, because country custom says you must feed all those men promptly at 12:00 noon. All food must be home-cooked. Fortunately, some of the neighbor Ranch Women feel it is their duty to help out in the kitchen.

While you nestle cases of beer and pop among the rocks at the edge of the creek, the men are furiously busy. Calves are cut away from their mammas, branding fires are started, ropers swing loops. Calves are roped and dragged, bellowing, towards waiting cowboys who grab the north and south ends of the poor little things and stretch in both directions. Other cowboys leap to apply the hot iron, castrate the little bulls, notch the ears and gouge out nubbins of horn.

You and the other women not smart enough to stay in the house, are in charge of the vaccinating, the tally sheet, the disinfectant, the scour pills, the blood stopper powder, and keeping track of the de-horning spoons.

The watchword for the Ranch Woman wielding any of the branding day implements is "Look Out!" Exude confidence as you approach a calf captured firmly by north and south cowboys. Have the vaccine gun ready. Pinch a bit of skin away from the calf's rib cage just under the foreleg. Thrust the needle in, making sure you don't poke through one side and out the other of the pinch, thereby squirting the vaccine in the air. Move quickly and try to keep out of the way of the man with the hot iron who is searing the brand into the calf's hide at the same time you are doing your needlework. The second

you've finished, remove needle and turn nonchalantly away.*
(see footnote) While being nonchalant, do not dawdle. Those
two cowboys holding the calf will turn loose all at once. Being
struck by flying hooves can take the enthusiasm out of the day.

About your person, hang a small notebook and pencil.
Dangling from the belt on the hipside of your leg is a handy
spot. Remember to tie these items on. Merely stuffing a
notebook and pencil in your pocket won't do. At the wrong
moment it will fall out and into a fresh juicy pile. Fish it out
and use it anyway. As each critter is vaccinated, it's up to you
to tally heifer or bull in your little book.

When you tally the bulls and heifers, you always get mixed
up, but NEVER admit it. Always answer promptly and
confidently even if you have to make it up.

Once or twice a lull occurs in the feverish activity. The men
sag against the corral posts or flop on the ground, beer cans
in hand. At this point, race for the house, make sure the big
coffee urn is full and functioning, check the roasts, stuff a
bushel of potatoes in oven to bake, mentally count the chairs
around the dining room table, and decide some people will
have to eat from laps in the living room.

Then race back to the corral where the thoughtful husband
has saved you one last swallow of warm beer.

At the noon break, pick up the bucket of Mountain
Oysters** (see footnote) and dash for the house ahead of the
men. While they "wash up", load the food on the table. No
matter how starved, the men will politely hang around outside
in the yard til you ring the come-and-get-it-bell. Once seated,
absolutely no sound is heard for the first ten minutes besides
the clinking of the eating utensils. When the first panic
subsides, limited conversation begins to trickle around the
table. By dessert, the morning's funny episodes and
catastrophes have been repeatedly analyzed and all bachelors
have been teased about their girlfriends.

---

* Caution: Although nonchalance is the key attitude, alert attention must be
the Ranch Woman's prime mover.

** Mountain Oysters: Those items separated from the bull calves. To be
laboriously cleaned, egg-battered, crumbed, and deep fried at a later date. Old
timers claim they're delicious as well as having certain rejuvenating powers. It
is not a good idea to dispute this claim.

Naturally, you and the other women, keep the coffee pot pouring and serving dishes full. Between trips, you get to eat, standing up, in the kitchen.

PART TWO:

GOOD OLD SUMMERTIME

SUMMER: That time of year when one is impossibly busy, the ranch bursts with life and company from the city descends in voracious hordes.

SECTION ELEVEN: SUMMER IRRIGATION

Wherein one learns what it is to cope with hired irrigators, husbands who work dawn til dark, and what potions and lotions to apply to cracked feet and blistered hands. One also learns about irrigating boots and how to reply to those dudes who want to know if you're goin' fishin'! And wherein one also learns how to hold the irrigating shovel.

"As early as possible" is your husband's motto regarding irrigation. That is—early in the spring and early in the morning. Some ranch operations retain a year-round hired man who is then available to help irrigate, if he doesn't quit. Since yours is a family operation, your man enlists your instant expert services. As summer develops and daylight extends, more and more time has to be allotted to irrigating. Finally, your man has to go to town to hire a hand. He may come home with anything from a broken down sheepherder to a high school kid. In any case, you exchange some (but not all) your irrigating privileges to devote more effort to the care and feeding of hungry men. This is not necessarily an improvement in status.

Irrigating and haying are two ranch activities that increase a man's appetite threefold while slimming down that bit of a paunch he developed over the winter. Sadly, while your husband slims down on the extra work, sweat, and food, you are apt to increase in girth.

Whether you have old, young, lazy, competent, or incompetent irrigators, all of them sweat. As a good ranch wife, encourage bathing and salt intake. With every meal, set out a giant bottle of salt tablets. The men will swallow these readily. Take some yourself also.

Those men who do not believe in bathing, become pungently noticeable. Be very careful about hints to bathe. If the man feels insulted, he may quit. And your husband prefers a stinking good irrigator to doing without help. A plentiful and frequent application of room spray may be all you can do.

As a thoughtful Ranch Wife, fill several canteens or waterbags so the men can carry drinking water. Likely they

will forget them. When thirsty, an irrigator drops to the
ground and sticks his face into the ditch, just like you see in
western movies. For some reason, irrigators never fall ill from
drinking ditchwater.

When your man strides forth in his seven-league irrigating
boots, his shovel balanced on one shoulder, and his hat pulled
low over horizon seeking eyes, he looks truly impressive.

The picture you present is a trifle less romantic. Irrigating
boots are rubber monsters that chew your poor burning
blistered feet relentlessly. The tall rubber things extend
halfway up the thigh, but are worn flapped over to reach just
below the knee. You are forced to walk slightly aspraddle.
Wearing your tacky oldest straw hat, packing a shovel and
walking spraddle-legged, you look a little like a chubby
peasant off to the ricefields.

Probably one of the most important things to remember
about irrigating is how to hold the shovel. When walking from
place to place, the proper carrying method is to angle the
shovel across one shoulder. At intervals, you must dig little
gullies to divert the water to spread over the pasture. Or you
have to spade up some sod to block the gullies because that
part of the field is wet enough. After gully digging, you are
required to spend a moment thoughtfully studying the
progress of the flow. At these moments, use the "Water
Watcher's Stance." Hold the shovel handle at the top end by
both overlapped cupped hands about chest high. Angle the
spade end out in front of you to rest in the dirt. Spread your
feet slightly in the "at ease" position. Viewed from the side, it
appears the shovel handle is propping up your body. The
"Water Watcher's Stance" is also the ready-for-action
position. You are ready to jab, spade, or scoop wherever water
needs to be diverted or dammed.

As you cross the county road where it separates the west
hayfield in half, watch out for two predators—rattlesnakes and
weekend fishermen. Both are harmless if dealt with decisively.
Every year one or two rattlers sun themselves right at the edge
of the culvert where it carries the ditch water under the road.
Do not hesitate or debate on the ecological balance of nature.
Kill it. To kill a rattler, bang it viciously with your shovel.

When it uncoils and tries to slither groggily off, jab down hard with the sharpened shovel edge, and cut off its head.* (see footnote) Cut off the rattles as soon as you're sure the thing is dead. Your oldest son is collecting them.

Sometimes as you cross the county road, a shiny car, obviously from the city, slows to a stop. A shiny man leans out and inquires how the fishing is. Remember it is not legal to do away with tourists or fishermen. Smile your simplest country smile. Then direct him to a fishing access, instruct him to close all gates, and to refrain from parking or picknicking in the hayfields. Then pull out your fisherman's log and take his name, address and license number. If he gets mad about giving his name, he'll roar off in a cloud of dust. Which means you wouldn't have wanted him anyway. Those who are friendly enough to chat and part with their names often turn out to be fine folks, and will even give you part of their catch.

On the long march home, you wish you hadn't forgotten your waterbag. At the house slip gratefully out of those nasty rubber boots. All summer long, both you and your husband will suffer from blistered, cracked, burning feet unless you take precautions. Daily, apply bag-balm liberally.** (see footnote) On top of that, apply cold cream. In addition, powder the insides of the boots. Lastly, pour a glass of iced tea from the big pitcher stashed in the refrigerator. Sit down and read for ten minutes before you get up to start dinner.

* Several blows may be required. The darn things are tough.

** Bag-balm: A soothing salve used to keep the milk cow's udder and teats soft and smooth. May be purchased at the local Farmer's Co-op.

SECTION TWELVE: HAYING

Wherein one learns to accept as normal, the preparation and serving of mountains of food to hay crews, and how to haul a snack to the fields. Plus advice on operating the tractor, the swather, the baler, and the mower, and make it appear that you know what you're doing.

Haying is that picturesque country activity indulged in by ranchers and farmers every summer. A clear blue sky arches over ripe yellow grain fields and lush green-gold hay meadows. City dwellers drive up and down the country roads in their air-conditioned vehicles and point at the sweaty men and growling machines.

Foot by foot meadows are mowed and the shorn grasses raked into windrows. Or if the swather is employed, the grass is cut and swept into even windrows without being raked. Then along comes the baler to eat the windrows and spit them out as haybales. Eventually, row upon row of bales dot the crewcut fields. After that, the farmhand* (see footnote) bucks the bales onto those beautiful haystacks the city folks admire as part of the summer scene.

Sometimes as a preliminary to cutting or swathing the meadows, your man will hitch the mower to the tractor and ask if you have time to "trim the ditches." Of course you have time.

Mowing the ditch edges first, helps more important and more expensive machines gauge how near they are to the ditch edges. A mower is a long toothy thing that sticks out sideways from the tractor. Sharpened teeth lie in a double row horizontally to the ground. As the tractor moves, pull a certain lever and the teeth gnash back and forth sawing through the tall grasses. There are several things you are not supposed to do when operating a mower. You're not supposed to slice rocks, small trees, fallen logs or jam the end into the side of the ditch.

At other times you may be asked to operate something

* A farmhand is not a person.

called a "side delivery rake." You are inclined to interpret that as meaning rakes give birth to little rakes on one side. That is not true. And don't mention the thought to your husband, especially if he's behind schedule.

The rake is employed on those areas where a mower has cut the entire field, generally a small patch where the big swather couldn't maneuver well. The rake scoops up the mown hay and "side delivers" it into windrows. It is considered OK for the Ranch Woman to operate a rake.

Rarely is the Ranch Woman called upon to run a swather.* (see footnote) Swathers are fun because you sit high, grandly chomping down a whole field. The thing has great huge circular teeth that look like the bristles of a super carpet sweeper. A swather cuts and mashes the grass and sweeps it into windrows all in one operation. The mashing process "conditions" the hay so that it cures faster. However, the beast is apt to suck up and mash dead skunks, pigeons and other deceased varmints. When the undescerning baler comes thonking along, it picks up and squeezes grass and varmints all together. (Breaking open a bale containing a rotted animal can be a pungent experience.) With the swather, avoid all the pitfalls you should have avoided with the mower and the rake. In addition, it's very important not to drive into the bog. A swather stuck in the bog is guaranteed to drive a good man berserk. Whether you could help it or not has no bearing.

In fact, a bog-stuck Ranch Woman better have a good excuse. The thinking Ranch Woman has a stock of good excuses prepared, such as: "had to avoid a boulder which would have broken a wheel;" or "had to avoid a kill-deer's nest of young ones;" or, best of all, you were "following the exact line set out by your husband to avoid falling in the bog."

When mowing, swathing and raking are completed, two or three days must elapse before baling to allow the hay to "cure" in the sunlight. If it rains, cursing and teeth gnashing ring out across the land.

The machine thing with the rythmic bang-thump-bang is called a baler. Growling like an angry dinosaur, it picks up the

* You only operate the swather in cases of severe emergency such as your man having two broken legs. Men adore swathers and guard them jealously.

windrows of grass and sucks them into its craw, then spits a string tied bale of hay out its backend. If you are drafted to run the baler, your neck will develop an awful crick from trying to watch fore and aft all at once. Watch ahead for rocks, pitfalls, and deceased varmints. Watch behind so that you know the baling twine is feeding through and tying the bales properly. The tension should not be too loose or so tight the string breaks. If a choice is necessary, it is better to bale a varmint than to break the darned string in the middle of the operation.

But you are always willing and eager to operate the machinery anytime. From your perch on top of the world, you have peace to compose letters to friends, to sing songs, to develop a new pattern, mentally write advice to your congressman and watch the bald eagles swoop over the river. Be careful to pay some attention to where you are going. It's during your most beautiful thought that the bog will suck you under.

For a Ranch Woman the absolutely most important thing to learn about machinery is the correct attitude. Approach and demeanor carry the day. Dress with a certain jauntiness. Jauntiness intimidates machinery. Wear your new straw hat and leather driving gloves. In order to avoid a patchwork-quilt tan, do not wear short-sleeved, open throated shirts. Haphazard tanning ruins the looks of your best white sleeveless low cut party dress. It makes your arms, brown to the vaccination scar, appear as though mismatched with your shoulders, while your neck and throat look as if you're suffering from a serious liver problem. High-necked sleeveless blouses are recommended, so that at least your face and arms tan evenly. On a hot summer day, the best garb of all is a bikini, if you can get away with it. Perched atop a machine, clad in your orange flowered bikini, work boots, straw hat and leather gloves, you present an arresting picture. Arrested is one of the things that will happen to you, your husband claims, if you don't wear something additional!

There is one chore everyone feels is more compatible with your talents. It's called turning the bales. Bale turning is particularly suited to you, say the men. Don't argue. Just advance to the field where about a million heavy bales dot the landscape. To make it easier for the stacker to scoop up the bales, they must be turned at right angles to the farmhand teeth. That part is pretty simple. It becomes more difficult when you have to turn the bales all the way over (a fresh bale weighs from 50 to 100 pounds) so that the down side is now up. All that is so the hay won't rot from the morning dews soaking into them before they reach the haystack.

While turning bales, wear something cool, but not your bikini or you'll be spiked to death from the spears of hay. Wear leather gloves, a straw hat, and tie a jug of water to your waist. Choose your own style of bale turning. Some folks like to start on the perimeter of a field and go in ever diminishing circles. Others prefer to march back and forth, gradually evening up the field. Upon reaching the center of the field, or your last bale, whichever comes first, sit on it, and have a big draft of water. Contemplate the bales that you should have been counting as you went along. If you've lost track, just decide on a number you think is close. WARNING: Bale turning can be hazardous to health. If you live in snake country, it is possible some of the creatures will seek out the cool underside of a haybale for a siesta. In addition to the water jug you carry, tie a stout forked stick to your belt. Fix it so you can grab it quickly. Usually the snake, startled at the interruption of his snooze, will try to slither away from you. Immobilize him with your stick then dig out your pocket knife and cut off his head and his rattles. Ignore any squeamish feelings about executing the snake. Better a little squeamishness than to wonder where it wandered off to.

The cruelest part of a haying operation is the stacking . . . for you anyway. Some very robust Ranch Women can maintain the lift, throw, push and pull pace of stacking with no ill effects. You, on the other hand, barely refrain from screaming as the pain increases in your back, arms, legs and feet. Even your eyes and teeth hurt. But you climb once again to the top of the stack because you'd die before admitting you are past your endurance.

Bale stacking technique is not difficult to master. Your man bucks up the bales with the farmhand, a wide thing applied to the front of the tractor. Several five-foot teeth set about twelve inches apart extend from it like bristles. The monster looks like a huge comb big enough to groom a pine tree. It scoops up a bunch of bales and carries them over to the stack atop which you stand. At the push of a lever, the teeth rise straight up to your level, then tip forward to dump its load. Grab the scattered bales (don't fail to bring along your bale hooks) and shove and push and lift into place. Stack one direction one row. Change to the other direction on the next row. Alternate directions all the way. No matter how tired you get, be alert when the farmhand growls up with a load. Being buried under an avalanche of heavy bales is awful. Besides, your man considers it time wasted to stop and administer first aid.

Both the haying crew and the stacking crew consists of your husband, a possible hired man, your son, and of course, you. Throughout all haying operations, there runs a terrible sense of urgency. The hay has to be cut before it's too ripe, then it's got to be baled before it rains, then it's got to be stacked as soon as possible.

As a good Ranch Woman, your main job is to keep the food, (food production is still considered your main job) drinks and salt tablets going. Often ranchers will hire a hay crew or one rancher will help another. No matter how it's done, you will have extra ravenous mouths to feed. Basic rules are simple. Prepare plain food and lots of it. Start each day by sticking a roast, a giant stew, or several chickens in the oven. At the right time, add potatoes and always make buckets of gravy. Salads and vegetables of any kind will do as long as they're not fancy. The men won't eat those dinky things with the sauces. Provide plenty of bread, butter and gallons of coffee . . . always. Cool drinks are acceptable as an addition, but never as a substitute for coffee. You can't miss with ice cream and cookies or cake for dessert. Buy the ice cream in five quart plastic buckets at the store. Always save the plastic buckets to fill with your own homemade ice cream when time permits. The buckets also make handy containers for holding nails, slops, or collecting eggs.

Mid-morning and mid-afternoon are key moments during haying season. As a noble, good, loving Ranch Woman, you ride to the rescue of the thirst and hunger crazed men at those times. Which means you cheerfully interrupt what you're doing to cater snacks to the fields. As you arrive toting your load, the men observe you immediately, but always make another round before pulling to a stop. This is to indicate they're ALMOST too busy to halt for a snack. However, never has a hay crew been known actually to refuse a snack. Amid a great deal of brow-wiping and complaints about the heat, three-fourths of a cake, a jug of ice-water, koolaide and a big thermos of coffee disappear. Then, at a secret signal, the men all rise, thank you profusely, each pulls out a used toothpick from a shirt pocket and remounts the swather or the baler or the rake or up on the haystack. This is all done in one concerted movement, leaving you standing or sitting among a scrap-pile of coffee cups, cake crumbs, and thermos jugs. You will have a distinct feeling nobody even knows your name. However, bravely tidy up and trudge home because it's almost time to start dinner.

On the days when you are drafted to run a machine, nobody gets any snacks, unless you prepare them ahead and take them to the fields with you. A snackless day is a day of moaning.

SECTION THIRTEEN: MOVING THE COWS
TO SUMMER PASTURE

Wherein one learns that you, as an incompetent instant hired hand, can lose a calf, but it takes an experienced cowman to lose a bull. One also receives lessons in correct vocabulary to employ while on a cattle drive, as well as the reason for starting the drive before dawn.

Sometime after the grass has greened up, your man squints at the sky, scuffs the ground and eyeballs the critters. In that mysterious intuitive way, he ascertains it is TIME TO MOVE THE COWS. Which means all the mamma cows, along with their children, must be gathered and pushed over the hills to the upper section.

On the evening before the magic day, your man casually remarks, "You have time to help ride tomorrow?" Of course you have time. You wouldn't miss it no matter what. Even pregnant, you can ride til you're six months along provided you don't fall off. Long before dawn, about 3:30 a.m., rise, and whip up a huge breakfast. In there somewhere make about a thousand sandwiches, several jugs of coffee and toss in a bunch of apples, cookies and/or cake. After breakfast pack the lunch. You'll have plenty of time because it'll still be dark for quite awhile. Ranch men rise in the middle of the night in preparation for a cattle drive. This is a ritual developed by men folks to the tune of noble grunts and groans, not to mention creaking bones. The men stagger forth to sit around the breakfast table drinking coffee and waiting for daylight.* (see footnote)

The food, the coffee, and some horses are loaded into the truck and unloaded at the Otter Creek corrals, three miles across the hills. From here, your husband, your son, the hired man, sometimes a neighbor or two, and you will begin the drive.

You haven't been on a horse since last fall's roundup and

* Waiting for daylight is a habit afflicting only men. It has something to do with being tuned in to the universal male rhythm of life—if you want to get silly about it.

both you and your mare could use some pre-conditioning, especially around the hips. However, as the sun rises high enough to be able to discern cow shapes from tree shapes, the two of you make a charming western picture against the morning skyline.

You are directed to gather "those cattle over there" and "don't miss any of the coulees." "Over there" encompasses a half section of sagebrush hills and rocky gullies. Pull your special cowboy stetson down snugly, but at a flattering angle over one eye and commence. Ride up the ridges and down the draws, swing into the brushy bottoms and check behind every outcropping of rock. Gradually you will gather several pairs of cows and calves. Patiently head them up the draw where the men are gathering critters from other directions.

Look to the right and admire your man as he expertly turns a spooky calf back to the herd. Just then that wild-eyed little brockle-faced calf in front of you ducks aside, zips around your horse, and gallops madly down the coulee—away from the herd. Kick the mare into a lope and try to circle wide around the calf. But the critter stays just ahead of you. As he suddenly disappears around a small hill, boot the mare into a gallop and cut over the top. If your strategy works, you will be ahead of the calf. He stops. You stop. Gradually and slowly ease towards the calf. If you can get him pointed the other way, he will tear back to his mamma. It's a matter of pride, honor, and fear not to lose that calf.* (see footnote)

As the calf stares at you, his eyes roll up as though having a seizure. Jumping a foot straight up, he lands running—in the wrong direction. Do not hesitate. Spur your horse. You've got to cut him off before he reaches the fence bordering the road. There's an underpass there used by the cattle to pass from one side of the pasture to the other. If he ducks through that he'll have a section and a half of unimpeded territory. Your poor chubby mare begins to wheeze and so do you. But you're both game. The mare, sensing victory, puts on a burst of speed. The calf, sensing freedom, also puts on a burst of speed and

* When a man loses a calf, it's a matter for comparative discussion about how snakey the little cuss was. If YOU lose a calf, it's due to a lack of attentiveness, ability and brains.

whizzes through the underpass. Ears flattened in anger, your wheezing steed pursues. The fact that the underpass is barely higher than the back of a horse could be a worrisome factor, if you thought about it. This is not the time for thinking. Cleave closely to that bobbing horsey neck and hang on. On the other side, open your eyes and regain control of your mount. At this point the calf is a half mile away, so let the damned thing go. While returning to the herd, use the time to prepare a good strong story, practice your nonchalant air, and don't ride too close to your husband for awhile.

Don't feel, no matter what your man implies, that you're the only one to let an animal slip away. As the trail gets longer and hotter, that big black bull with the froze-off ear, heads for the brush. Your man pushes him out of the creek bottom three times. Where a fence line sweeps over the little butte, the old bull disappears. While the rest of you ride on, your man rides to find the bull. Half an hour later, your husband, the experienced cowman, rejoins the group of cowboys and cattle—without the bull. Do not ask any questions. Eventually you will learn the true adventure tale of how the bull escaped into the thorn bushes. The tale will grow with the telling until the bull develops into an incredibly foxy old so and so. How to capture such an outstanding bull becomes a hot subject for awhile.

Whenever a cow critter decides to go her own way or becomes balky or hangs back she is urged forward on the path of righteousness with some well chosen words. These words describe her ancestry, her moral fiber, and her attitude towards life. Most of the words need only four letters to spell them. As a good Ranch Woman, ignore all of these verbalizations. The men are barely aware of the pearls falling from their lips. Rich descriptive vocabularies are always part of a cattle drive. You don't condone the language, but are not above an occasional sizzling comment. The time the old horned cow bunted your horse and caught you in the knee cap, your man, the hired hand and two neighbors regarded you with respectful awe.

At the end of a couple of hours of riding, cows and tired calves crest the last ridge and spread out over the new seeding your man planted last year. The green grass almost brushes the cows' bellies. It's a fine sight to see next year's income happily munching away.

Dismount along with the men and take a few moments to loll. Although the men hunker, it's better to put your knees on the ground and sit back on your heels. Hunkering is a manly art not recommended for women.* (see footnote)

Lolling time over, the men make noises indicating they're about to mount up. This is the signal to crawl in the saddle and get a good fast head start. Lope the mare over the hill and descend to the creek bottom. It's the only brushy spot for miles and your physical problem is becoming more and more urgent. Toilet technique while on a cattle drive in open country with male companions can be painful. Usually, when you begin eyeballing every little rock and sagebush, one of the men chooses that moment for friendly discussion. (They've ignored you for over three hours up to that point.) A selected team of Ranch Women researched this particular subject. The objective conclusion reached was that male persons simply don't HAVE to as often as female persons. In the event that a male person DOES have to, he merely rides apart, stops his horse and dismounts to adjust the cinch. Turning casually away (on the far side of the horse), he spends a moment scanning the horizon, his clear eyes ostensibly searching for critters. In just a little while he apparently finishes scanning, mounts up and proceeds with the cattle drive.

Things aren't quite so easy for female persons. One method is to take along a camera. When the moment becomes desperate and you can't get rid of a male companion, announce you want to take a picture from "over there." Tell him to "ride on" so you can obtain a cowboy rider in the photograph. Then dash for that clump of sagebrush. If you can stand it, take the picture first.* (see footnote)

When you finally ride down that last draw and see the Otter Creek corrals spread out below, you decide you'll live after all.

* If you try to hunker, your legs cramp and your feet go to sleep. Rising smoothly becomes impossible. You're reduced to rolling forward on hands and knees, then clambering awkwardly and painfully upright.

* It doesn't matter whether there's actually film in the camera.

Everybody dismounts, bone tired, dirty, sweaty and played out. The men tie up the horses in the shade and flop down alongside. You, of course, go to the truck and begin to unpack the sandwiches.

After a huge intake of sandwiches, coffee, and dessert, the whole crew revives slightly. Relax blissfully flat on the ground and listen as the men describe and explain and remark about each cow, the remarkable growth of the new grass seeding, and how the loco weed isn't so bad this year. Contentedly pull your hat over your eyes and slip peacefully off to sleep.

SECTION FOURTEEN: VETERINARY CARE

Wherein one learns how to haul a sick critter to the vet. One also learns what to do while the veterinarian delivers a calf by Caesarean section.

Survival of farm animals in pre-vet days must have been sketchy. It's the worst kind of discouragement to watch healthy, bouncy calves, piglets or lambs sicken and die. Often the little creatures expire seemingly for no reason at all. Sometimes the disease that carries them off can be identified and sometimes not. A common killer of baby animals is called "scours".* (see footnote) Before penicillin and antibiotics, farmers and ranchers tried a remarkable variety of cures. Only the strongly constituted survived. When a critter got sick, it got better, or it died.** (see footnote)

A veterinarian serving a rural community talks little, but is endowed with incredible courage and hardiness. At any hour, and in any weather, he will come to a critter's aid. Unlike people doctors, vets still make barn calls. However, they do charge mileage.

When an animal is sick, it is more convenient (and cheaper) to take it to the veterinarian's office where he has proper tools and equipment. Hauling a sick critter to the vet frequently falls to you, as chief towngoer. This is especially true if it's a baby animal.

On a snowy, cold morning towards the end of winter, it becomes necessary to haul a sick bull calf to the doctor. In the back of the station wagon, your husband spreads a large piece of canvas. Leave a pre-cooked meal available if possible. Otherwise the men will have bread, butter, and huge bowls of dry cereal. The bowls will be piled neatly in the sink, pathetic testimony to their avowed inability to "cook".

Domestic chores under control, climb in the car and start

---

* Scours: a general term for that loose bowel condition that comes in a variety of colors. However, mustard yellow is usual.

** An old time remedy for scours: "Take a piece of bright colored yarn and tie around the calf's tail close to the root."

towards town. It's best to keep in mind your husband's last words, "drive carefully." It has begun to snow harder, the flakes coming down in soft, wet clinging globs. The little bull calf lies behind you flat on his side, twitching and shivering, eyes showing white. All goes well for several miles. The calf is too sick to do anything but lie there. Suddenly he begins to blat and flop his head about. Speak soothingly. The soft tone won't do much to calm the calf, but it will make you feel better. As you round that rather sharpish curve halfway to town, the calf rolls sideways. The motion stimulates him to activity. He struggles to his feet. Wobbling and lurching wildly from side to side, eyes rolling, tongue lolling, the calf emits a horrendous bawl, right in your ear. Do not let this bother you. Concentrate on driving, alternately viewing the calf's actions in the rear view mirror with peering through the snowy windshield. As the calf lunges over your shoulder, bawls in your ear, and drools down your back, reach with your free hand to push him back from time to time. Don't, however, startle him. At all costs, keep his front end facing you. Creep the remaining distance to town, one hand lapped over the back of the seat, ready to push on the calf's brisket when needed. The last few miles become an exercise in bearing pain. Circulation has ceased in the cold fingers of the hand fiercely gripping the steering wheel. Neck and shoulder muscles are steel bands painfully tensed against a possible forward rush of the calf. The arm and hand half twisted over the back of the seat is about to dislocate at the shoulder.* (see footnote)

Eventually, you reach the sanctuary of the vet's office. Gratefully pry yourself loose from the steering wheel and try to reorganize kinked muscles. The Doctor, a kindly intentioned man, asks if you have a problem. Refrain from comment on the obvious as you hold the door while the Doc attempts to capture the calf. The reluctant and terrified patient is transported by hand to the treatment room. Once the Doctor flops the calf onto the treatment table you are called upon to assist by holding things down. That means four legs, a head and a flying, fecal saturated tail must be kept under control.

* During this sort of medical emergency, all Ranch Women develop a third arm and hand. No one knows how.

Drape yourself over the calf, octupus fashion, taking care the tail doesn't pull free to flap in either yours or the good Doctor's face. While you maintain a four corners control, Doc administers medication. The sick calf is usually dehydrated and must have something intravenously. While the cheerful veterinarian arranges the intravenous set up with its tubes and bottles, maintain your close relationship with the calf. Try to achieve a mutual trusting rapport because Doc expects you to hold the calf still while he inserts a giant needle in a vein. Should you suddenly begin tossing and jerking, there's an even chance you too may receive something intravenously.

Whatever treatment is applied, it smells like rotten effluvium. The nasty odor clings to clothing for days. Finally, the Doctor is finished. He scoops up the calf and carries him to the car while you trail behind carrying a bag of those same smelly potions to be administered at home. The short parade is met at the door by Mrs. Super Rancher, her face arranged in greeting. Actually, she greets Doc, who (still holding the calf), courteously responds to her questions. She tosses you a conversational morsel by mentioning how well you look and that HER husband wouldn't expect HER to haul a sick critter to town.

Smile and pass on by. She'll never notice for a while, that glob of fecal material clinging to the back of her pale beige coat.

Sometimes the veterinarian must come to you, particularly if a heifer has to have a Caesarean and it's too late to haul her to town. Your husband prepares a clean stall in the barn and spreads around a generous layer of fresh straw.

When Doc arrives, the heifer is suffering, her breathing labored, her sides heaving. She must be encouraged to lie down. Using a system of rope loops, the two men throw her down, left side up, as gently as possible. In fact, they don't even cuss much around a cow in labor.

The cow's front feet are tied together and then the rope anchored to the side of the pen. The action is repeated for the back feet with the holding rope then hitched to the opposite side of the pen. When the cow is trussed so she can't kick, there remains another portion of her to control, especially if she's fidgety. Your husband and the veterinarian look at you and state, "OK." Which means you now move to the cow's head and sit on it. (It's helpful to remember that cows only have teeth in their bottom jaws.) Sit facing the operation zone and more up on the neck than actually on the head itself. You're fortunate if she's a cow without horns. She can't do much in this situation, but every time you look around, she's staring at you. When she catches your eye, she moans and her eyeballs roll wildly.

As soon as the novacaine takes effect, the vet makes a long incision in the mother's side. While the doctor works, you don't have a lot to do except become educated.* (see footnote) Your man, meanwhile, is preparing the resuscitator, which is a thing that blows oxygen into a calf's lungs while sucking out phlegm and mucous from its throat. As soon as the newborn emerges, the doctor and your husband work quickly to get the little critter breathing. If no resuscitator is available, alternate methods include draping the calf by his hind legs over the top rail of the stall, or swinging him, nose down while holding him up by the back legs. While the holding and draping operation is going on, (fortunately you don't have to do that—unless, of course, you're the only other person there) your job is to insert a tickling piece of straw up the calf's nostril which causes him to sneeze and thereby blow out the phlegm. Naturally, you have removed yourself from the cow's neck to engage in the tickling procedure. Once that calf is out of her the mother seems to relax a bit.

When the calf is breathing well, you and your man rub him briskly with a clean rag and work his front legs back and forth. After he's dried off, help him lie down so his feet are under his body. Don't let him lie on his side in order to avoid danger of those fresh new lungs filling with fluid.

Finally, the operation is completed. The calf looks fine. The mother is relaxed, the gash in her side stitched tidily together. Your husband and the vet release the holding ropes and untie the cow's feet. She pops up as though nothing had happened,

* Attending a Caesarean is not a good idea if you are squeamish or pregnant yourself.

walks over to the newborn child and begins licking.* (see footnote)

All the people leave the pen. Scrape the crud off your coveralls, thank the vet and invite him to the house for coffee. He thanks you and states he'll be along in a minute. As a good Ranch Woman, take your cue and leave. Your husband stays behind to help Doc gather his gear. In the course of gathering, your spouse extracts a bottle of medicinal spirits concealed in the tackle box.* (see footnote) The two men then drape an arm each over the top rail of the stall, take a couple of medicinal pulls from the bottle, and commence to discuss the operation, mention the calf is "pretty big for a Caesarian", and comment that there seems to be more Caesarians this year than ever before.

Eventually, you observe them advancing towards the house. Have coffee and cookies ready. As you pour the coffee, add a short splash of household medicinal bourbon to each cup. Make this a very obvious gesture. Place the bottle in the center of the table next to the cookie plate. Then stand back and watch the peculiar glances the men exchange with each other.

* Old experienced cowmen always break in young aspiring cowhands by telling them their job is to "lick off the green calves."

* In certain situations, a Ranch Man exhibits amazing forethought.

SECTION FIFTEEN: GARDEN MAINTENANCE

Wherein one learns to name weeds by their Anglo-Saxon subtitles. One also learns the true aggressive nature of peas, beans and all those other garden vegetables. Advice offered on how to Tom Sawyer the cucumbers.

A major part of summer is spent grubbing about in THE GARDEN. Watering, irrigating, weeding, and hoeing are words used to describe a sore back, blistered fingers, mud-caked clothes, and a feeling of black panic when it all begins to get away from you.

By the end of summer your entire body falls easily into the hoe-handle stance. The other favored position is the hands and knees crawl. The crawl position saves your back and allows you to notice from close up which plants have bugs. A drawback is the discoloration of knees. As you crawl, the moist earth grinds through the layers of coverall and blue jean to press into the pores of the kneecaps. Your knees develop a mottled, slightly diseased appearance. It doesn't matter much until wearing a short dress, you have to sit in the front row at Woman's Club.

Try to maintain a sense of humor when leafing through the gardening magazines and seed catalogs.* (see footnote) Those magazines always feature elegant spiffy ladies dressed in white denim Italian tailored outfits with coiffured hair peeking out from under expensive garden chapeaus. Grandly they stand there, holding gleaming clean garden trowels, while wearing cute little garden gloves untainted by any specks of soil.

The garden picture you present contains some variations from the ideal. However, do not be dismayed. Garden costuming is important to summertime morale. Each summer, buy a new dimestore polka-dot or patterned straw hat with a chiffon ribbon. Approach the garden wearing your new hat, striped bib overalls, your old red rubber high school rainboots and old stained thin leather gloves. Except for the mud, the

* Leafing through magazines is done while performing one's ablutions. Knowledge of current affairs would be unavailable to ranchers and farmers if it weren't for bathroom libraries.

freckles, the broad beam, and the can of mosquito spray clutched to your person, you too could pose for an ad. Mosquito spray or lotion is an absolute must. As your garden grows, so do the mosquitoes. Always wipe, spray, or douse with repellent any part of you that is exposed before charging the garden. Early morning and late afternoon hours suit your schedule best for gardening. The mosquitoes know this. They train and sharpen their stingers during mid-day. Should you run out of repellent, used motor oil is an excellent substitute.* (see footnote) Both the oil and the repellent stink, but should you be asked to pose for a magazine, the smell won't print.

Plan to weed daily. Plan for your sons to weed daily. Press any passing neighbor kids into service as well. Use force, threats, blackmail, bribery, wheedling, coaxing, cajoling or any other ploy you can think of to get the weeding done. A constant supply of cookies, koolaide, and iced tea should be available to the weeders.

Chickens and geese can be drafted to help kill weeds and bugs. (However, it is not necessary to reward them with cookies or koolaide.) Banty chickens are especially good at eating slugs. Show a banty a slug and general excitement ripples through his or her little body. Soon the whole gang zips here and there gobbling up the yummies. Geese eat quack grass and any kind of weed. Take care they don't start on the lettuce leaves, however. It's best to let the geese help garden only when you're there to oversee. Geese automatically fertilize as they garden—about every five seconds. When bored with eating, they tend to congregate at the front door where they fertilize the front steps a lot. At all times be aware of the location of the geese. Encourage them to work at the opposite end of the garden from you because geese are basically sneaks. Geese attack anything or anybody from behind. Your standard garden posture offers the foul birds an easy target.

As your garden grows and grows, it becomes evident you are going to have to DO something with all that produce. Some items like lettuce, spinach or radishes bear early. Eat a lot and

* Ordinarily the motor oil is used on the pigs from a contraption known as a pig-oiler.

give a whole lot away. Take basketsful to the old folks home and the Senior Citizen Center. Freeze all the spinach and swiss chard you can. It tastes good in cold weather, is full of healthful iron, and helps maintain regularity.

As the garden ripens more or less all at once, you can stand in the middle and hear the plants shouting and pleading in a frenzy of emotion to be harvested. Apples ripen, corn is ready and berries are falling off bushes. There's a distinct feeling the garden is uprising to come after you. Do not panic or fall into a fit.

At the edge of the garden, station an old table or a bench or a plank on two sawhorses. On top, keep two or three colanders handy, covered with plastic for cleanliness. Have the garden hose available. As you pick the produce, wash and rinse it right there on the table. Place the washed stuff in the colanders and take to the house. On the stove, a giant pot of water is boiling. (All ranch and farm women learn that "keep the pot boiling" is not merely a useless old saying.) On the back burner place a potful of water—fresh daily. Whenever you head for the garden flip on the burner. When you come in, the water is hot and ready to go. Blanche the vegetables you've brought in with you, drain and stuff into plastic bags and drop in freezer. Pick, blanche and freeze as fast as you can because canning season is racing towards you. If you are the particular type, follow any cookbook for length of blanching time. Otherwise, merely slosh the leafy stuff til it wilts and boil the hard poddy stuff til it turns bright green.

As cucumbers ripen, they go crazy. Eat as many as possible and make pickles from the rest. If yours is a pickle loving family, you may not skip pickle making. The thing to do is to find several town ladies who may not have a garden but do enjoy making pickles. Offer these talented women unlimited quantities of cukes in exchange for a jar or two of pickles or relish or whatever they fancy to make. If the cucumber crop doesn't freeze out too early, you can acquire enough pickles and relish to last the family all winter.

SECTION SIXTEEN: VARMINT CONTROL

Wherein one learns that the beasts of nature are not on your side. One also learns how to get rid of magpies, 'coons, coyotes, foxes and egg-sucking cats.

On every ranch or farm, hazards, tragedies and misfortunes lurk in the form of drought, flood, freezing, rustlers and particularly, varmints. As a true Ranch Woman you develop a certain expertise in varmint control which means you learn to set out traps, bait and how to shoot.

For every domestic critter, there's a whole gamut of wild varmints ready to do him in. The coyotes and foxes eat the young lambs and then join the skunks to eat the chickens and geese. The raccoons kill the cats and eat grain from feed troughs, from the grain barrel in the barn or from the cob in the garden. Mice, of course, eat everything including the fleece lining of your saddle.

If none of the above cost you a year's profit, the city dogs suddenly band together and go on a killing rampage, slaughtering baby critters in berserk frenzy. If you survive all the natural pitfalls due you for that year, rustlers decide to relieve you of some of the burden of caring for animals.* (see footnote)

To combat the ravage of preying varmints, whether they be four or two-legged, the ranch or farm develops its own troops and armaments. Be fearless. Attend to varmint removal promptly!

To keep the mice population semi-controlled, every farm has many cats. You, as a thinking Ranch Woman, keep at least two housecats of the female sex. Once she's proved herself a good mouser, get her spayed. She'll stay home and skulk around mouse houses.**

Your man deals with coyotes and foxes, by setting out traps

---

* Rustlers either remove the entire animal or butcher it immediately leaving only entrails and tire tracks to mark the spot.

** If you're scared of some dark place, like the root cellar, take a cat with you. Throw her in first with instructions to search and destroy.

or poison depending on what the government is allowing that month. When coyotes are in the ascendancy, you may start the season with sixty ewes each with a frisky lamb or two by her side. As ravaging coyotes eat the babies, you stand helpless as the death count goes from ten to twenty to thirty to forty lambs. Profit is gone, meat is gone, wool is gone, but the coyotes are healthily producing litters of eight to ten pups a year—on a diet of your lambs.

Raccoons are difficult to eliminate, partly because they're such cute, furry, black-masked animals. Both sons acquire one or two as a pet at least once. The morning comes, however, when you step into the garden and find all the ears pulled from the cornstalks and the tomatoes ravaged. Harden your heart. It's you or the 'coons. You must permanently remove those crop destroying varmints. Be brave. (That means pleading with your husband to shoot, trap, poison or imprison the creatures.) Try leaving a good dog in the garden at night with instructions to scare away raccoons. This is chancy because he may abandon his post or sleep through the party. A raccoon can be discouraged from eating ears of corn by putting red pepper into the top of each ear. If you've got half an acre or whole fields planted in corn, you're going to need a lot of pepper and a lot of time and a lot of nose tissue while you work. This is an excellent theory (they say) and works well until it rains.

Magpies are beautiful birds that abound. Handsome sturdy creatures, they sport a white breast, black head and tail feathers with gleaming blue-green highlights. A magpie is also a thief, scavenger and cannibal. Magpies dive bomb the song birds off their nests and eat their eggs. They also eat grain, dog food and your rosehips left out to dry. They fly boldly into the chicken coop, spear an egg, and fly off, egg and all.

Liquidate these winged wonders with a .22 or a shotgun. Your oldest son is happy to sharpen his marksmanship on magpies. You, however, shoot badly and don't like to anyway. But there are days when you would strangle personally any magpie you could catch. Be of good cheer. Your chance is coming.

On a warm drowsy afternoon when the chickens are all out of the coop, you notice a parade of magpies walking like black suilted businessmen into the chicken house. Naturally, you are preparing to leave for town dressed in your best hot pink pants suit. But you do not hesitate. Instantly reach for that old hardwood axe handle you keep behind the woodbox. Carrying the handle, keep cautiously out of the line of sight and tippy-toe up to the chicken house.

Cautiously open the door, slip through and shove down the panel over the chicken exit hole in the bottom of the door. Look about and note magpies clinging to the upper corners of the coop staring at you and growling.* (see footnote) Growl back and wave your club. As the birds hysterically swoop past your head, flail about with it. (WARNING: When a particularly aggressive bird flies straight toward you, be careful. A mighty swing can miss the bird and clonk excrutiatingly on your own forehead. Your presence is required at the bake sale as coffee-pourer in town. When you show up late, sporting a huge purple protruberance over one eye, no one will swallow the story about magpies being responsible.)

You may or may not manage to down all the magpies trapped in the coop. As their numbers dwindle, the last one or two seem to get the message. They cling to the top corners and refuse to fly within clouting range. However, it won't hurt to let a couple of them escape. The survivors apparently carry the word back to their relatives. For quite awhile, magpies steer clear of the henhouse.

Skunks present another pungent problem. In spring, the dogs and sometimes the horses, acquire a delicate perfume. If at all possible, plead with your man and son to deal with skunks. It's best to trap them alive. Your husband has developed a skunk catching box that has only the door opening and one small round hole in the roof of the box. After capture, he inserts a piece of hose from the skunk box to the exhaust pipe of the pickup. Then he starts the motor. Exercise selectivity and judgment in attending to skunk removal and burial. Many ranches have small, well removed gullies or coulees named "Skunk Hollow".

* Pay no attention to persons who claim birds don't growl.

Porcupines can present a prickly problem. If possible bait them into a box and relocate miles away. Should you be faced with the necessity to kill a procupine, don't. Call your husband and refuse to think further about the problem.

Occasionally an outlaw cat becomes hooked on raw eggs. Craftily, the feline felon sneaks into the chicken house, punctures an egg and laps up the goodies. It's easy to tell which cat is the culprit. He's the one with the lustrous sheen to his coat who sits in the sunny spot in front of the chicken house licking himself and smiling. If Barney, the egg-sucking cat is tame, round him up and give him to a favorite relative as a loving companion. If Barney is wild, it may become advisable to execute him. Again prevail upon your husband.* (see footnote)

As with other of the basic raw facts of nature, it is not necessary to dwell on varmints and especially their executions in conversation, particularly around town folk or ecologist types. Should you, for some reason, find youself harassed by such a person, send the person a nice live magpie in a cage as a gift.

*Since your husband hates to have to kill anything almost as much as you do, super-rich chocolate cakes are the order of the day at these times.

SECTION SEVENTEEN: SUMMER COMPANY

Wherein one learns that otherwise polite friends who live in the city tend to look upon you, the Ranch Woman, as recreation leader for THEIR vacations. One learns some methods of ridding oneself of unwelcome visitors.

Summer company differs from standard drop-in visits of neighbors and friends. Neighbor folks "stop by" on a particular errand or to visit about interesting news such as the weather, the crops, the twin calves or the upcoming Community Hall Dance.

Summer company has traveled from AFAR in order to visit someone who LIVES IN THE COUNTRY. They have scheduled your ranch or farm as part of their yearned for summer vacation or week-end jaunt.

Summer company consists of persons of slight acquaintance and distant relatives so far removed, intermarriage would not be a problem. Somehow they've developed a sudden close warm personal yearning to be near.

As a good Ranch Woman, you will often devote summer Sundays to the care and feeding of company from the city. When the Sundays extend to a week or more, you will plumb your depths for patience and tolerance. This Saintly approach will mainly drive you plumb dippy before summer is over.

Generally, summer company arrives in a family package: a man, wife, from two to six children and a pet dog. (Always a big German Shepherd or a neurotic toy canine of some sort, or both.) None of the group knows anything about the country. But my, oh my, are they enthusiastic!

"So wonderful to breathe the fresh country air," they burble, as the dog roars out of the car and rips off a chicken. (You, naturally, assure them that it's all right—it was just an old rooster—as your best laying hen gasps out her last.) The visitors seem convinced the entire countryside has been unrolled for their special pleasure during weekends and vacations. After that it's all rolled up again and put in storage til next year.

In summer, you, as the good Ranch Woman, will struggle

out of bed anywhere between five and six a.m. (or earlier). That allows plenty of time to prepare breakfast for your husband, family and the hired hands. Then trot out to feed the chickens, the pigs and the bum lambs before trotting back to the house to fix breakfast for THE COMPANY. The company pull themselves out of the nest from eightish up to noonish.

Country custom says your job is to be cheerfully chatty as you serve up platters of "real country breakfast." That means lots of eggs, bacon or sausage, and hotcakes with two kinds of homemade syrup. Smile when Mrs. Mother Company has to cut ten year old Junior's bacon and egg for him. Smile when nine year old Juniorette loftily refuses her portion of breakfast and demands cornflakes. Continue smiling when the dear child sprinkles out twelve flakes into a dish, smothers them under a half cup of sugar, then drowns everything under a flood of cream. Smile, when after two bites, Juniorette decides she doesn't like all that cream, takes five cookies from the jar and exits, leaving a globby mess strewn on the kitchen table.*
(see footnote) Keep smiling, but move swiftly to intercept Junior as he leaves, toting the bacon platter. His intentions are to feed the remaining eight pieces to King-the-Collie. (You had planned to dice up the leftover bacon into the scalloped corn casserole for dinner.)

Over the years, summer company falls into recognizable types. There is Type A: the loud-talking family group that never lets you know ahead of time they're coming. They pull into the yard unannounced, **always** at chore time. They've been "sight-seeing" in the nearest city a hundred miles away for three days, but hadn't thought to call ahead. Naturally they expect to stay for supper and overnight lodging. (You pray it's ONLY overnight.)

Type B: the barely acquainted or never heard of persons referred to you by mutual "friends." The "friends" are generally old army buddies of your husband's or former co-workers from that summer your man worked in the oil fields before you were married. Or they know his or your sister in

---

*King-the-Collie loves summer company. Into his dish go all the yummy cream leftovers and half eaten eggs. In addition, he usually manages to steal at least one kid-cookie per handful.

Peoria. Country custom says you must find beds, sleeping bags (you hope the little kids in bags won't wet) and floor space for all.* (see footnote) As the company start up the walk, throw your dish towel over one shoulder, go to the door, and welcome them cheerfully. Mentally calculate the increase in hungry mouths and break out the card tables for the kids to eat from. Sit up late that night exchanging conversational trivia. Find out early whether the visitors plan to leave next day or are preparing to camp with you "for a few days." If it begins to look like you may have the pleasure of their presence for very long, start lacing the conversation with comments about how bad the rattlesnakes are this year. Mention your near-heart attack when you reached for the mop bucket and disturbed a big snake at least eight feet long. Describe how it hissed and struck at you, narrowly missing your hand. If young children are among the group, mention an outbreak of a new strain of measles in the area. Add that your son has been exposed and you're a little worried because there's no vaccine yet developed for this new measle bug.

Type C company includes relatives—close, and relatives—distant. Close relatives, such as in-laws tend to stop by during those times when there's already a houseful of company. Feeling somewhat deposed, the in-laws are inclined to snub the already entrenched company. Conversation at the dinner table drags to a halt as you and your husband try desperately to introduce a subject of interest to all. Immediately after the meal, your man dissappears to work on the tractor, doctor the calves, or check the windmill. For whatever reason, he fades away leaving you with two groups of persons talking at you, but not to each other. As soon as the dishes are finished, (by you, while the company watches) put on your coveralls, grab a shovel and invite everybody to help clean the chicken house. Whether anyone helps or not is immaterial. By the time you get back to the house, at least one of the company groups will have decided to move on.

Type D company includes those relatives or friends who are

* Ranch and farm houses are expected to come equipped with foldout, foldup, bunk and trundle beds tucked away in various crannies.

rich and/or imposing. Your husband's Aunt Bertha, whom he hasn't seen in ten years, always sends the kids expensive Christmas presents accompanied by long letters of helpful child-raising advice. On the worst possible day, Auntie Bertha phones from the local country store for proper directions to the ranch. Obviously there's only one thing to do, short of running away from home. Instruct her carefully in ALMOST the right direction. With only a very small slip of the tongue, you can steer her left instead of right at the crossroads. By the time she stops and asks and backtracks, you will have gained perhaps a whole hour to GET READY. Last week's company, including four kids, just left and you haven't had time to do any picking up. Therefore, the house is carpeted wall to wall with a mixture of toys, rock collections, picture books, clothes, and a chaotic jumble of unnamed THINGS. Do not panic. Take a deep breath and scream once to clear your head. Then concentrate on scooping up the clutter and stuffing it into closets. Hastily run the vacuum around the middle of the rooms. Quickly swish-wipe the bathroom and dust the guestroom. Open the package of brand new sheets kept for emergencies only and apply to guest bed. Stack all the dirty dishes in the dishwasher. What's left over, put in brown paper sacks and shove under the sink. (That night after Auntie retires, fish them out and wash.) Race to the yard and pick some sort of flowers. Jam them in the crystal vase you're pretty sure Aunt Bertha gave you several Christmasses ago, and place it on the dresser in the guestroom.

Just as you finish the fastest cleanup in the West, Aunt Bertha drives into the yard, where she is first greeted by four big white Canadian geese, honking and hissing. Arrange your smile, carry your dishtowel, and go out to welcome Aunt Bertha. IMPORTANT: Carrying the dishtowel is an absolute must. It is a dual purpose implement. Besides giving you something to wring other than your hands, it can be employed to discipline a friendly seventy-pound collie and fend off honking, hissing, wing-flapping geese. Aunt Bertha cringes before the snapping onslaught, whereupon the geese press the attack to bite her nyloned legs.* (see footnote)

As the summer progresses, the guest traffic increases, particularly if you are on the route to a National Park, the World's Fair or own a saddlehorse. All city people "rode a horse when they were little." Such past expertise equips them to "round up the cattle." Whether the cattle should be rounded up has no bearing. The company wants to do something "typically western." This includes riding, roping, shooting and eating. It excludes hay-stacking, irrigating and manure shoveling.

Common to most types of summer company is an obsessive urge to PLAN. They'll try to fit into two weeks every scenic wonder possible. You are drafted as the local guide and social leader to "show them the sights." Which means you must plan two days' meals for your family in advance. Leave the butter churning til you return, along with the separator washing, the garden watering, weed pulling and canning and freezing chores. If you mention these duties in a desperate effort to stave off the inevitable, the company gaily dismisses them all and urges you to "take a day off and relax." They claim they will help you upon returning. (They won't. They're always too tired.)

However, give in gracefully, because your husband is craftily urging you to go also. Even though there will be extra chores for him, he would rather see you herd the guests out of his way. This allows him time to get his farming, or haying, or some other major project underway without interruption from "helpful" company.

Helpful company can drive a good man batty. For three days, your husband has rescued greenhorns from being mashed by a tractor, trampled by cows, and drowning in the irrigation ditch. One entire evening was spent searching for the company's German shepherd who had gotten himself lost while following his horseback-riding master.

Be a good Ranch Wife and take the guests off on a trip,

---

* Don't forget upon entering the house with Aunt Bertha in tow, to discard the now goose-soiled dish towel. Aunt will remind you if you forget. Make an obvious show of selecting a fresh, clean towel.

leaving only Cousin Agnes behind (who sprained her ankle yesterday when she fell off the corral fence). Upon your return, you will find that Cousin Agnes has helpfully cleaned all your kitchen cupboards She has also efficiently reorganized your entire storage scheme. It's been a year now and you still haven't found everything.

As summer draws to a close, you think you can begin to relax. School opens in a week. After that people have to stay home with their kids. Be thankful for compulsory schooling. Enjoy your few moments of solitude. Just around the corner is hunting season when hordes of hunters will be turned loose upon the land—generally yours.

SECTION EIGHTEEN: CANNING, FREEZING AND "PUTTING UP" ALL THAT GARDEN PRODUCE

Wherein one learns that mother nature can overwhelm. One also learns that frontier life without electricity and freezers must have been hell.

To be a Ranch or Farm Wife is to be afflicted with an overpowering urge to can. NOT to can all that produce would cause an unbearable burden of guilt. Therefore, beginning in midsummer, you, as a True Blue Ranch Woman must drag out the canning kettle, the pressure cooker and a million jars.

Even thinking about canning causes a sticky footed lurch to your step as you remember the gluey, syrupy mess from spilled over and boiled over liquids. The easiest way of preserving food is to freeze it. Anything will freeze, but sometimes the flavor or texture is changed in the process. For example, it is not a good idea to freeze lemon pie, as it tends to taste like frozen sawdust. Generally, a working combination of canning and freezing is employed when preserving food.

Lurking in the storage shed and fruit cellar, are baskets and boxes of empty fruit jars, jelly jars, odd bottles, and interesting glass containers.* (see footnote) Clustered in the top kitchen cupboards, never used ordinarily because they are too high to reach, are more bottles and jars of assorted sizes and shapes. But no Ranch Woman has enough jars. Each year the need for more increases until your husband becomes convinced you're a jar addict. Jar collecting is, however, merely a desperate and futile hedge against the avalanche of fruits and vegetables that must be "put up." Somehow you have a feeling that if you collect enough jars, canning won't be so bad this year. But it will be. Canning will be bad this year and next year and on and on forever.

There are two periods of time within the twenty-four hour

* The fruit cellar, over the winter months, has become a hatchery for creepy wild life. Spiders and bugs dangle from the roof beams, while you're positive an unseen monster is skulking in the black hole behind the potatoes. It's comforting to take both the cat and the dog along. At least they'll raise an alarm if something grabs you.

cycle that are best for canning. At these times, other humans and all animals are quietly asleep. Only you are astir, cackling softly over your brews. Early morning is the favored time choice for many, oh very early. Stagger out of bed by 4 a.m. at least. The other time slot preferred by some Ranch Women is the ten p.m. to one a.m. shift.* (see footnote)

Whichever time you choose, remember to PREPARE ahead. Clear the kitchen table, the counter tops, and every surface in sight of the usual litter. Place canning kettles, or pressure cookers on stove. Have plenty of long-handled wooden spoons at the ready. Line up a stack of boxes of fruit jars on standby alert on the back porch. On the sink counter, have washed, scalded and turned upside down on clean cloths a multitude of jars. Be sure you have plenty of lids of the correct size!

There is no way to make canning really fun, unless you hire someone to do it for you. The canning season usually begins with berries. The juice has to be extracted and canned and later made into jellies and syrups. Having picked gallons and gallons of whatever berry is presently ripe, dump them in the biggest kettle, cover with water and heat to boiling. If you are fussy, carefully wash and pick out extraneous leaves and bugs before heating. However, a few stirs after the kettle begins to heat will bring all that floating to the top. Then you can skim most of it off. What's left won't hurt the flavor and you're going to strain it all anyway.

For just how long to cook what and which method to use, consult any good canning and preserving book. It won't be long before you will have every step memorized as you can things day after day after day after day, ad nauseum.

Sometimes when you've nobly risen at 4 a.m. to fight the canning battle, you find yourself having visions of South Sea islands where the food drops off trees. Or you find yourself making up limericks having to do with banning canning. Or stray lines from the dim past when you read Shakespeare, flicker in your mind. As you swirl your wooden spoon among the vapor clouds emanating from the giant kettle boiling on

* Be careful not to sit down in a soft chair during the evening shift. To do so is to fall asleep. At which point whatever is cooking immediately boils over.

the stove, you find yourself muttering something about "bubble, bubble, toil and trouble." Generally, just at the moment when you're really getting into the swing of the recitation, complete with eerie cackling, your man stumbles into the kitchen for his morning cup of coffee. Peering at you through the mists, he lifts his cup to misquote solemnly, "a rag, a bone, and a hank o'hair; by God, there stands my lady fair." It's best to accept this bit of humor in the vein in which it is offered. Burning your finger on the kettle and bursting into tears helps also.

Early morning canning sessions aren't too bad once you've conquered the pain of getting up and getting started. Late night sessions, however, can be more exhausting. As the hour grows later, the mountain of food to be canned seems to increase. Your feet hurt; your back aches. As you stare at the bubbling cauldron, you wish to God the entire outfit would blow itself up. Somehow you feel that would put an end to the whole canning question.

During the late night sessions, as the hour grows later and tireder, it is recommended to take two aspirins and a glass of soda pop. In the bottom of the glass, first pour in a heaping shot of bourbon. If the pain in your back, legs and feet does not diminish within 15 minutes, add more bourbon.* (see footnote)

A pardonable habit of all Ranch and Farm Women is to march any visitors down to the basement or out to the root cellar to show them the rows and rows and rows of shining jars of canned tomatoes, green and yellow vegetables, fruits, jellies, syrups, meats and pickles. Each jar is neatly labeled with its year of birth. You are filled with satisfaction and pride as you view the display. Insist, therefore, on hearing admiring oh's and ah's from your visitors. Mention how much you will be saving on the food bill and how good home canned food tastes as compared with that plastic store stuff.

Often, it is well into fall, before you can bear to disturb those rows of sparkling jars. Once an inroad has been made, it's no time before there's practically nothing left and you are again facing armies of empty jars waiting to be filled.

* Exercise caution with this remedy. The aim is to blot out your physical pain without dissolving yourself.

SECTION NINETEEN: SUMMER FUN

Wherein one learns the correct method of country tippling and how to dance country style.

Summer dances in the country are held at Swamp Creek Community Hall. The occasion truly enriches your life while debilitating your system. You drive to the Hall in the pickup. Important preparations must be made. A cooler filled with soft drinks, ice cubes, paper cups and beer is fitted in on your side of the pickup underfoot. The hard liquor is kept in the glove compartment. Make heaps of sandwiches or a giant, heavily frosted cake to carry into the dance hall and place with other donations in the Hall kitchen. At midnight, you and the other wives will lay out the food and pour the coffee—just like home.

The cooler and glove compartment items remain AT ALL TIMES in the pickup.

In the Hall itself, the men congregate in a bottleneck at the front door. Wooden benches lining the hall support long rows of women and children. You sit on a bench and "gab" with the other women.

From time to time, small groups of men quietly leave the Hall and casually head for the vehicles. Later on, the departures and re-entries become noisier while the dancing markedly increases. No realistic Ranch Woman can expect actually to dance for the first two hours.

You are introduced from time to time to other ranchers and their wives. Not necessarily by name, however. "Like you to meet the wife," or, "have you met my woman?" is about as close to hearing your actual name uttered as you can expect.

At midnight, a line of hungry noisy revelers clomp past the food table, where a large commandeered cowboy hat is held by a large commandeered cowboy who collects money from the men to pay the musicians (always two quitars and an accordian).

After food intake, the ranch men settle down to serious drinking and dancing.

Country custom says you must dance every dance as long as your strength and feet hold out. Try not to shudder at the piercing war whoops which now punctuate the end of every number.

Since midnight you have refrained from drinking hard liquor. If the bottle is passed to you, only pretend to swallow since at four or five in the morning, SOMEBODY has to be sober enough to drive home. As a true Ranch Woman, you are a proficient driver of any style vehicle.

Always, on the eve of the Annual Rodeo, the whole of any country town turns out to drink, dance and catch up on local news. Every bar and every fraternal organization holds a "dance" with "live" music. Which means anybody who can play at least three tunes on a quitar qualifies as a musician. Drinks are served in paper, styrofoam or plastic cups at all the liquor emporiums. This convenience allows imbibers to port their drinks into and out of bars, across streets and up and down sidewalks. The imitation glassware does not break, thus saving feet and fingers from possible laceration. Bar operators do not have to replace smashed or lost glass inventory and the town doctor saves on bandages.

In country towns, no one arrives at a dance before 10 p.m. Animals must be tended and chores must be done first. As dusk settles in, your husband "gets ready to go to town." His going-to-town-clothes consist of clean levies, shirt, no tie, his "dress" hat and his fancy pair of cowboy boots. Your costume is much the same except you don't have to wear a hat unless you're competing in the rodeo queen contest. Or you may yield to a certain nostalgic yearning and wear a dress. Whatever your choice, always remember to wear low-heeled comfortable shoes or boots.

During much of the evening, you stand around holding a drink and watching all the other people. No ranch or farm man ever sits down at a public dance. Along with other levi-garbed males, your man bottlenecks in the doorways to watch other folks, listen to the musicians and "visit" with his neighbors.

As the evening progresses and your feet play out, you learn to develop restful leaning methods. Lean for awhile against your husband. Then lean for awhile on the juke box, the piano, or the pool table. If you ever get near the bar, lean on it. When the eddies of people carry you near the edge of the room, it's quite restful to double one leg and prop oneself, storklike, against the wall. Glance into any country bar late on a festive night and you will see a lot of apparently one-legged women lining the walls. While this position can be restful, take care lest the doubled up leg goes to sleep, causing possible collapse as you try to walk.

Some years the town fathers and bar owners decide to have a street dance. Down the center of the block of main street, sawhorse tables blossom. Each end of the street is closed to car traffic. Bar owners haul out basic liqour supplies and ice in washtubs. At intervals up and down the sidewalks, musicians station themselves to play country music.

There's something about a street dance that drives otherwise sane and sensible farmers and ranchers slightly mad. During the festivities it is best that you and your husband develop a strategy. Take standing positions in the shelter of a doorway next to a bar. Usually there's music in the bar as well as on the street. So your chances of getting to dance are increased.* (see footnote)

For weeks and months after a street dance, the countryside resounds with wild tales, most of which are true. Legends are born and sometimes politicians are elected on the basis of campaign behavior on rodeo eve.

Such was the case with one of the county commissioners recently re-elected. After careful consideration and half a quart of whiskey, the would-be commissioner decided to pass around his campaign cards. Accordingly, he saddled his old white mare and proceeded to ride her around and around the block long street bar, passing out cards and handshakes. He also accepted drinks whenever offered, which was not infrequent. The inevitable occurred. It struck the campaigner that the people INSIDE the buildings were being deprived of his cards. Methodically, the aspiring politician guided the mare into every bar and dance hall in town. Solemnly, he

* Even more important, you have access to a ladies' room. No matter how liberated, it is not a good idea to slip down an alley. Not so liberated men are apt to be lurking there with a similar chore in mind.

proferred cards to people seated in booths, dancing couples and those going to and fro. It was while crossing the dance floor at the fraternal lodge hall that the mare became nervous and deposited some business in the middle of the floor. Amid roars and shrieks of laughter, the horseback politician pulled his steed to a halt to view the somewhat steamy pile behind him. As the laughers quieted slightly to regain their breaths, the commissioner rose tall in his stirrups, swept off his hat, and proclaimed, "Folks, if you want your business done right, vote for me!" He was voted into office by an overwhelming majority and has held the post for eight years.

Lucky is the Ranch Woman whose spouse can and will dance. Likely though, you are among the vast sisterhood of Ranch Women Yearners. As the music pours over and around you, the yearning to really dance becomes an actual pain. Every person in the room moves to the music except for the contingent of ranchers clumped in the doorway and captained by your husband.

Generally, you are driven to desperation and have to implore and plead. Surprised at such an odd request, your man dutifully escorts you onto the dance floor. Having reached a location he likes, he commences guiding you about more or less in time with the music. Duty done, he again takes up his vigil near the door, satisfied that you've had your fun.

There are some gems among ranch men who truly like to dance and actually go about inviting the ladies! Be sure to get on that man's list for at least one twirl. That will make two times for the evening anyway.

As the liqour consumption increases, the clots of men stationed in doorways begin to filter onto the dance floor. Like sleeping bears, the men rouse to the music.* (see footnote) For awhile you find yourself whirling and stomping around the room with a variety of partners. You must be brave as you adapt courageously to the varied dancing forms.** (see footnote)

*Imbibing all that firewater helps, too. The trick is to get in as many dances as possible before the men get thirsty again. Or before they become so inebriated they can't maneuver.

** Those low-heeled comfortable shoes mentioned earlier should also be STURDY!

Although styles vary, basic country dancing is always the two-step—sometimes slow and sometimes fast. The two steps can be two steps forward and back, or two forward and forward, or backward and backward or from side to side. While two-stepping, you are piloted around the floor or across it. Your feet follow your partner in whatever direction he's going, while your right hand is clasped in his left, in a grip as if he's hanging on to a snakey critter. Those two clasped hands often describe a rhythmic pattern not necessarily related to the music or the two-step. Sometimes your hand and arm is lowered and raised from knee level to shoulder with each drumbeat. Sometimes your partner caroms at a gallop around the floor. You, of course, gallop along, too. Holding your hand in his, in rigid extension, your partner uses the pair of stiff arms to break trail through the thickets of people. Hang on tight to his shoulder with your remaining hand. The galloper is usually programmed for one direction only and you're bound to be dizzy before it's all over.

Country custom says you may not refuse a dance request. Besides you wouldn't want to. That surfeit of dancing won't last long before the men disappear to quench a desperate thirst again.

PART THREE:

FALL

FALL: A gorgeous and beautiful time of year when you can't believe summer is over. The critters grow lots of hair and a great deal of energy is spent discussing MARKET PRICES.

SECTION TWENTY: ROUNDUP TIME
AND MARKETING THE CALVES

*Wherein one again becomes an instant cowpoke. Wherein
one also learns that the stockyards are a man's world and after
an hour, remarkably boring.*

As the ranch swings into the rhythm of the fall season, the
animals grow sleek and shiny. Calves begin to change from
fractious funny youngsters to stocky cud-chewing cattle. A
short, but peaceful, lull of good living, good eating and good
health pervades the ranch. Then one day, that smooth ribbon
of peace develops a crinkle. MARKET REPORTS blare over
radio and TV. Your husband listens intently to fast talking,
twangy-accented announcers, auctioneers and cattle buyers
singing their market songs. Dire predictions fall from your
mate's lips. Gloomily, he searches for reassurance but without
real hope.

Listen sympathetically as he worries that the calves will be
too light to bring a good price. Remain calm as he fidgets
waiting to see if prices will go up. Don't argue while he
gloomily predicts the bottom will fall out of the market. Cluck
compassionately when he says he won't be able to buy feed for
the cows and pigs this winter. But it won't matter because he'll
have to forfeit the place to pay the bills anyway.

As a good Ranch Woman, do not mention any activity that
costs money. Try not to have dental problems, mechanical
failures or terminate pregnancies previous to marketing the
calves.

Keep a supply of old envelopes on the kitchen table so he
can "figure."* (see footnote)

The morning finally arrives when your man decides it's time
to bring in the cows and calves. The kids stay home from
school and a couple of neighbors sign on to help out. At an
unreal hour in the predawn (about three a.m.) you serve

* For a ranch man, the backs of old envelopes are first choice for figuring
anything. After that it's paper napkins, the edges of newspapers or the insides
of match covers.

breakfast to the entire bunch of cowhands.

As a thinking Ranch Woman, make several pots of coffee the night before and stir up a giant batch of hotcake batter. Country custom says the pancakes should be "sourdough." However, fiddling around with all that may be more than you can stand previous to the drive. Don't say anything. Simply build the pancakes with buttermilk. Make the batter a little thin and put in lots of baking powder, a little sugar, but NO soda. The cakes will be puffy, golden and taste a trifle sour. Drop the word "sourdough" once or twice and all will gulp the cakes with relish. To cinch your reputation as an early morning hostess, add a few blueberries to the batter. Serve the usual vast quantities of eggs and bacon and keep the coffee coming.

In a flash, the mountain of breakfast is done away with. It's still a long time before daylight. The men can't start to gather the cattle because they can't see. They've gotten up early in order to "get ready" to ride, which means sitting around the breakfast table discussing market prices and drinking coffee (which you pour).* (see footnote)

Eventually, a thin grayish tone sifts into the sky. It's possible to discern faintly the outlines of the garden gate through the window. The men comment upon this phenomenom for awhile. At a secret signal they all rise, clap hats on heads and go out to saddle up. Your dear husband saddles your mare for you, thus giving you time to clear away the mess from the table and put last minute things into the oven or refrigerator.

There's an old tradition in some western circles which says everyone saddles his own mount. That includes women in particular so it won't appear a man is "waiting on" a woman. If ever your man subscribes to this sentiment, it can leave you frantically clearing up the kitchen, racing for the barn, hurriedly saddling up and galloping after the men. When you catch up, you're apt to be greeted with clever remarks about being late or the way you bounce when you ride. Clearly, the thinking Ranch Woman must devise a subtle hint to

* You personally are never actually noticed as a living being. The only reality is the coffee pot attached to the end of your arm.

encourage chivalry. Therefore, the moment the men leave, quickly don your riding boots, jacket, hat and gloves.* (see footnote) On your way out the door, stop by the kitchen table. Do not—repeat—do NOT remove a single object! Leave dishes, syrup, leftover eggs, ketchup—everything. Gather up the four corners of the tablecloth. Bring them together and tie a nice knot. Grasp the bundle firmly and tote to the large incinerator which stands on the path between the house and the barn. Drop bundle in incinerator. Calmly continue to the barn and saddle your mare. Later that day, let your man discover the deposit. When he asks, "Why??!" (he will certainly do that) mention sweetly that for you it's either cleanup or saddleup. (This is a can't fail recipe.)

An air of tense frustrated hurry permeates the early morning roundup. The cows and calves have to be corraled. Mammas and offspring have to be separated and the calves trucked to loading corrals outside of town by ten o'clock to meet the BUYER. Separating cows from calves is not always a smooth operation. After the critters are herded together in the big corral, the men deftly edge them a few at a time towards the small corral that is the anteroom to the loading chute. Your job is of prime importance. It's up to you to handle the swinging gate leading into the small corral. As a cow-calf pair heads your way urged forward by grinning No. 1 son, you must open the gate at the proper moment, let the calves slip through and quickly slam the gate closed in the cow's face. Sometimes you miss, and both a mother and calf enter your gate at once. Be prepared with a special curse word at this point. If you do not feel comfortable using hard core swear words, develop a repertoire of substitutes in French or Russian. You will need something vehement when a heavy pole gate reverberates off a thousand pound cow to slam back on you. As a satisfactory expletive, "naughty, naughty" just won't do.

It's always a half hour late when the calves finally reach the rendezvous point. There, the Red-Nosed Buyer has the option

* It's best to line up your own and the kids' riding outfits the night before. Boots, jackets, hats, and arms and legs can be difficult to find in the early morning.

to accept or reject calves.* (see footnote) When prices are high and the buyer can turn all the critters he can get for a profit, he takes every calf without question. However, when it's a bad year and you desperately need the money, the buyer cuts back small calves, off-color calves, short-tailed calves, long-eared calves, or anything else he imagines doesn't look right.

In prosperous years, after the deal is consummated and the calves are on their way to a feedlot, your husband is likely to generously invite all the men who helped to have dinner and drinks at the local restaurant. (On him, of course!) In that event, you always go along and reign as Queen of the Mayhem. It's a double pleasure because it means you don't have to cook and serve meals to all those people—or clean up after them!

Some years, your husband prefers to haul the calves to market where they are sold at auction. The same routine prevails as regards rounding up in the dawn's early light and feeding everybody breakfast.

As soon as the calves are sorted, abandon your gate duty and race for the house. You have previously organized your "town" clothes. Quickly change into that dressy pants suit, polished sand-colored boots, and smart suede leather coat your husband bought you for Christmas.* (see footnote) Add small earrings, (if you're the type), your posh, fawn-colored Western hat and don't forget mascara for the long-lashed look. In the city, putting on makeup comes first. However, in the country it's best to leave personal face beautification until last. Should you be required to hit the trail immediately, if not sooner, at least you'll be attired attractively. You can do your face in the vehicle while traveling. All ranch women learn to apply lipstick while riding in a two-ton truck over bumpy roads.

Eighty miles down the road, the caravan of vehicles full of calves arrives at the auction yards. After unloading, the men step into the "chute office." Country custom says you do not

* Cattle buyers come in tall, short, fat and thin sizes. For some reason (possibly due to the alcohol content in their systems) most of them have red noses. All wear expensive boots and hats which never get dirty. They are given to a lot of squinting and hand flapping as they accept or reject each calf.

* After you picked it out, clued in the salesperson and guided your man to the shop door.

enter the office with them, but hang around outside. Pay no attention to custom. Go on in. All over the office walls are various nekkid women calendars and interesting semi-dirty signs. Look demurely at the floor as your husband and the other men studiously avoid staring at the pictures of the unclothed ladies. After checking in at the chute office, the men form a loose cluster and mosey among the pens, eyeballing and commenting on the critters within. You trail along. From now on you are totally invisible. Yours is not to reason why. Yours is merely to trail along behind. At the sale ring, all climb to the top of the bleacher seats spread around three sides of the auction ring. Keep following. From past experience you know that the men are going to hang around the yards the entire day. Be patient. Escape is possible.

As the excited throaty voiced auctioneer rattles off unintelligible sounds, the men nod wisely. As for you, an occasional clicking of the tongue suffices. Add to that a small shake of the head and you may earn a reputation as a shrewd judge of livestock.

In the ring the animals keep coming and going through an entrance and exit door located on either side of the auctioneer's high booth. A man with a ten foot pole keeps the calves circling so all the buyers (who sit down front) can get a good look. Swirling sawdust, cigar and cigarette smoke, and flying excrement thicken the air. After a long time of wise nodding and tongue clickings, even the men develop a need for change.

Every stockyard has an eatery always named "Stockman's Cafe", or sometimes, "Stockman's Bar and Cafe". Rows and rows of vinyl plastic, flyspecked booths extend along the walls. The men fit themselves into a booth with you squashed in the corner. A waitress, wearing a too tight pastel uniform and giant dangly earrings, brings a pot of coffee and a stack of cups without being asked. She passes around the cups and pours the first round. After that, the men in the booth handle the job. IMPORTANT NOTE: Pouring the coffee in the Stockman's Cafe is NOT up to you. Don't even make the attempt! As friends and passersby stop at the booth to visit, your husband grandly waves the coffee pot about and invites them to join the party. HE pours the newcomer's coffee as well as refilling everyone's cup. Lastly, he notices you and bends the spout your way. At this point, cover the cup with your hand and whisper that you need to exit for personal reasons. Excuse yourself with a lovely smile to the assembled stockmen, tell your man you'll see him later, smile once more, and get the hell out of there.* (see footnote) Head for uptown. Visit the art galleries, buy school clothes for the kids, purchase an outfit for yourself, and have an elegant lunch in the tearoom. (Sometime during the afternoon, buy your husband a new shirt.) Rest assured your husband remains happily glued to the stockyards while you are cramming a year's shopping into three or four hours.

On the way home, you and your spouse exchange stories. While he relates the mysteries of the market, you describe your exciting afternoon. Always show him one of the new shirts you thoughtfully purchased for him. As you draw nearer home, begin a graphic discussion of food that includes juicy steak, baked potato and strawberry shortcake. Time the gourmet discourse to peak just as you crest the rise leading to the Country Inn Supper Club. (This is a can't fail recipe to insure a nice ending to the day over cocktails and a lovely dinner not prepared by you.)

* Naturally, as a thinking Ranch Woman, you have a duplicate set of keys to the truck.

SECTION TWENTY-ONE: GETTING IN THE WOOD FOR WINTER

Wherein one learns how to operate the chain saw, how to throw wood, stack wood, dump wood, and rick wood into neat piles. One also learns how to get wood hauled from woodpile to stoves.

It's been your privilege to notice that Mrs. Super Rancher lives in a super elegant ranch house where everything matches and is color coordinated. Her house is also uniformly heated by invisible electric or gas geniis. One or more super elegant matched rock or brick fireplaces with giant mantel pieces, room wide hearths, and glass doors, provide focal points around and against which tidy polished guests lean to sip toddies at five. Objet d'arts adorn the mantel.

Your own establishment has slightly fewer posh appointments, but does have wood-burning units in more than one room. The major unit provides central heating for the entire house. It's a funny looking brown baked enameled metal squarish thing about four and a half feet high that takes up an ungainly amount of space right in the living room. Rising like a black dinosaur neck out of its backside is a stovepipe which makes a right angle turn before disappearing into the chimney. The background behind the stove is not graced by decorative rocks or stone. Rather, painted sheetrock, smudged, merely stands there making a wall. The only objet d'art is a tin can one half full of water sitting on top attempting to pass as a humidifier for the room. Draped artistically atop the can may be a pair or two of cotton work gloves drip drying.

The other wood burning unit in your house is found in the kitchen. It's called a cookstove. It is a dual purpose outfit that provides heat for the kitchen and the back part of the house, not to mention that during the winter you cook on it to save electricity.

Both the living room and the kitchen stoves eat wood. Lots of it. The wood must be sought out, cut, gathered, hauled, stacked and eventually carted into the house. Most often this job is one accomplished by your man. Frequently, you get to help with wood gathering. Sometimes as need requires, you may go off into the timber on your own. Hitch the small trailer to the small tractor. In the trailer, place a can of gas and a can of chain oil, plus your own personal lightweight chain saw your man bought for you last Christmas.* (see footnote)

Although the subject of getting the wood in for winter has often been mentioned during the summer and early fall months, serious attention is not paid to the project until the first wet cold snowfall of the season. Dress and attitude are important in wood gathering. Wear a warm jacket over coveralls and stout leather gloves. Hat style is optional, but don't forget earmuffs. These last are a must. Earmuffs warm your ears and prevent incipient deafness from the roar of the chainsaw.

(If you are accompanying your man on a wood gathering trip, maintain a cheerful air of commaraderie. It's probably the first outing you've had together since haying last summer.)

When all is prepared in readiness for the sojourn, whistle for the dogs, mount your tractor and sally forth. Arriving at the timber site, dismount, remove your saw from the trailer and rev it up. To rev up a saw, grasp the pull cord and snap smartly, as with a lawn mower. Several snaps later, as with the lawn mower, go into a helpless feminine flap and get your man to start the darn thing. If he is not with you on the outing, shriek and curse and try again. In awhile it will start.

Woodsawing is the practice of cutting up big trees and branches into small lengths suitable for the cookstove and the heater stove. Neither great skill, impressive wisdom, nor absolute emotional stability are required to master the art. You will have no trouble. First, locate a nice, not too fat, deadfall tree. With your saw growling away, slice off the small prickly limbs and branches. Then dissect the somewhat thicker branches from the main trunk. After which commence to make big sticks into little ones. Make the tree trunk into logs. It's best to have a pair of wrap around goggles of some

---

* Do not scoff. A chain saw is a boon and a blessing to all ranch women. It's a little like the difference between a whalebone needle threaded with catgut and an electric sewing machine.

sort to protect your eyes from flying sawdust. (Usually you don't have or can't find them.) However, a piece of clear plastic wrapped across your own regular glasses and tied behind your head works admirably.

After a time of sawing, your machine runs out of gas. Fill from the gas can you've brought along, check the oil and fill that, too. Take time out to blow your nose because all that bending over makes the juices flow. If you've been particularly thoughtful and planned ahead, you've brought along a thermos of coffee. Pour yourself some and relax against a tree trunk to admire the sky and scenery. If you're very lucky, you will see several varieties of birds. Among the treetops bald eagles swoop and sometimes the flash of a bluebird startles your reverie. After awhile, bestir yourself to charge into the task once more. Use up one more tank of gas in the saw. After two go-rounds you've got a passle of wood pieces lying all over. Commence picking them up and throwing them into the trailer. You can use these moments to exercise and stretch your whole body by alternating arched over hand shots with underhand fast zingers. The extra bends you have to use to pick up the pieces that missed the trailer altogether will remove inches from the waistline.

Finally, refill the saw with gas and oil. Then place it carefully in its case and perch it, along with the gas and oil cans, on top of the trailer load of wood. Climb aboard the tractor and head for home. It's been a zesty afternoon. There is still, however, the problem of unloading, stacking and toting wood to the house. As you near home, stop singing. Park the trailerfull of wood by the woodpile. Put away your saw and equipment. Go into the house and start supper or have a nice hot bath.

The second you hear the school bus at the end of the lane, go to the door wearing an excruciatingly warm smile. Indicate the trailer load of wood and mention to number one son that a reward of a favorite dessert awaits. Instruct number two son to follow in his brother's footsteps. In no time at all, the boys have the wood unloaded and stacked. It's been a matter of but a few moments more for them to tote several armloads into the woodboxes in the house. When your man arrives home from the South 40, invite him to join the three of you for some milk and fattening chocolate cake. Remember to grimace slightly and hold your back in pain as you get up to pour him coffee. Mention how well the boys unloaded and stacked the wood YOU sawed ALL afternoon. Receive his commendations with a modest smile and offer him more cake. Maybe in the next week or two you can manage to get away for another afternoon of bird watching and wood sawing.

SECTION TWENTY-TWO:
CLEANING THE PIG SHEDS
(Also done in spring)

Wherein one learns the important step-by-step method of efficacious shoveling of pig manure.

When the leaves on the cottonwoods begin to think of turning from summer green to gold and tan, all twelve sow ladies begin to dream of baby piglets. The mamma sows waddle as their bellies grow plump.

As in the spring, the girls also farrow in the fall. Also, as in spring, the farrowing pens must be cleaned and made ready for the ladies' confinements. Although the task is not complex, it has a certain delicacy not suited to all women. Naturally, you enjoy it. Unlike house cleaning, diaper washing or oven scouring, preparing the pig parlor has a creative purpose. Besides, the pigs aren't critical.

On an auspicious day, attire yourself in bib overalls, a long-sleeved shirt and your polka dot baseball cap. Stuff your hair up under the cap or else tie a scarf, turban style, over your locks. It is also useful to wear a bandana around the neck. Pen cleaning is guaranteed to diminish the lustre of a Dior outfit. Wear cotton or leather work gloves and take along a thermos of coffee. Important: Load your pockets with a good supply of nose tissue. If you aren't allergic to dust before you start, you soon will be.

Approach pig pen cleaning with a philosophical whistle-while-you-work attitude . . . at first. After awhile the dust chokes off that sport. Besides your teeth become coated with grime, making it difficult to slide your lips into a pucker. As the air thickens, raise your neck bandana across your mouth and nose, bandido style.

Equipment for proper pig pen cleaning consists of a basic all purpose pitch fork, a garden rake, a grain scoop, a manure fork, a stiff broom and a wheelbarrow. Add to these a garden hoe blade that has no handle. It can be noted here that posh pork farms have cement block farrowing houses with cement floors, air conditioning in summer and circulating heat in winter. Neat cubicles house each mamma. No untidyness exists anywhere. Somehow posh porkers don't seem to chew up guard rails, bash in feed pans or defecate on their environment.

Your own setup can be described as folksy. The building was once a big horse barn in the days before motorized vehicles. The interior is divided by wooden panels into farrowing pens. All twelve pregnant Spot sows are a happy-go-lucky group, but destructive. Happily they'll leap onto a panel and smash it to bits or chomp holes in the walls and floors as they make nests. Each day brings a fresh broken panel to fix or a hole to board up. The final effect is a mish-mash of uneven boards, jagged-edged patches on patches, and temporary adjustments that remain there permanently. Definitely, your farrowing barn does not qualify for "Swine House Beautiful". But the pigs don't care.

Farrowing pens are constructed like big city efficiency apartments. The maternity room is at the back, the parlor area, kitchen and bathroom at the front. At one side of the maternity area, like a gutter space next to a bowling alley, is a narrow fenced-off space called a "creep". The creep allows the babies to cuddle up under a low hanging heat lamp, but prevents mamma sow from stealing all the piglets' water or baby pig pablum. A two by four guard rail eight inches off the floor and eight inches away from the wall lines the remaining sides of the pen. The guard rail prevents mother from inadvertently squashing one of the children.

When not in use as a farrowing hospital, the rooms are let to just any old pig who wishes lodging for the night. Over the several months since the last farrowing, there has been no maid service. Old, piled up straw and dirt and other natural refinements lie in thick layers and must be removed.

Therefore, after you get yourself lined out with appropriate tools and equipment, do not dilly-dally. Start with the largest forked implement and scoop up all the loose straw. Develop a rhythm. Singing an old plantation slave song sometimes helps. Scoop up, lift, and toss the treasure into the wheelbarrow. When the barrow becomes full, wheel it to the center aisle that runs between the pens and dump. Repeat as many times as needed.

(Later your husband gets to scoop it all up again and sling it into the spreader. You can help, but try not to. It's better to exhaust yourself pen cleaning. Or develop back symptoms. Or have a baby yourself. If at all possible, avoid loading the manure spreader. Heaving forkfuls of heavy stuff up above your head, and over, and into a spreader is a gruesomely painful chore.)

Starting at the back, scrape the bottom of the pen. Then sweep. Assume a kneeling position and use your hoe blade to get at the corners of the creep and pen. The entire pen cleaning operation, after some practice, should require about an hour per pen. However, time may vary according to how thick the crudd lies and how much help you have. Usually several dogs and all twelve sows are in the pen with you, busily searching for lost bits of grain.

Beware that a careless pig doesn't step on your hand as you kneel in a corner. Be prepared to scratch backs and rub sow bellies. But try to prevent an affectionate 600 pound sow in search of a belly rub from collapsing full length right where you are sweeping. Eventually the girls become bored with what you are offering for entertainment and depart for a nap. Succeeding pen cleaning goes a little faster.

Finally, all the straw, dirt and guck is removed from the pen. Next, go fetch the bucket of barn lime. A scoop at a time, fling the lime about the cleaned pen. Use a wide-armed sweeping motion as though you're pitching a horseshoe or taking a bow. Make certain the lime clings to the upper sides of the pens and take particular care to sprinkle thickly in all corners and along edges.

Last, and very important, close the pen gate and secure it with baling wire at both top and bottom corners. DO NOT depend on a new-fangled hooks, bolts or snap locks. Most sows have a special ability to pick locks and break fasteners. However, there is no recorded instance that any have learned how to untwist baling wire.

SECTION TWENTY-THREE:
THE ART OF OPENING GATES

Wherein one learns how to open and close normal gates as well as husband gates.

Sometimes women wonder about their rightful place in the scheme of things. As a Ranch Woman, you do not have that problem. Your place is at your husband's side—the right side—in the pickup, with one hand clutching the door handle waiting for a gate to appear. Poised and alert, your eyes constantly scan the road ahead, muscles tensed to spring into action. You are secure in the knowledge that you are NEEDED. As an experienced gate opener you are responsible for tremendous savings of gasoline, shoe leather, and extra man power. The energy conserved because of your special ability would subsidize an entire underprivileged nation.

After awhile you achieve an expertise in gate opening. In consultation* (see footnote) with other Ranch Women, basic techniques have evolved for coping with any style of gate.

Dress code for gate opening is any costume of the moment. However, gloves are a skin saver. Keep an emergency pair in the glove compartment of all the ranch vehicles.

Gate Type A: Consists of basic metal structures—two styles. The first are those slick, neat, aluminum or light steel things. Often painted green, these gates are a marvel of easy opening. To wrest wide such a portal is a cinch. As your man slows to a halt at a gate, assume a casual competent-ranch-person air, slip lightly out of the pickup and approach the target. Take time to admire the birds and flowers. At the gate, daintily flick upward a little U-shaped gismo that prevents the latch bar from emerging from its slot. Reach for the convenient balanced handle and gently pull. The latch bar slides back and the gate begins to move silently on velvet hinges. Smile and wave at your man as he drives through. Close the gate with the same satisfying elan.

Metal gate, style two, may require considerably more

* consultation: i.e., gab-session

emotional control and muscular ability. Usually, it's a metal
unit adapted from a former life, such as an old iron bedstead.
Frequently, the thing is a patched together assortment of pipe
and chain link units trying to pass as a genuine gate. Always,
sharp pieces of jagged metal, wire ends and weird rusty
formations reach out to slash and tear various bits off you. It is
now you will need those gloves.

Undo the fastener, which is always a rusty chain or a wound-
around piece of baling wire. The gate behaves reasonably well
as you grasp, lift, heave and begin dragging. Suddenly it will
spear itself into the ground, stabbing you on the chin as it does
so. Stop and spit on your gloved hands.* (see footnote)

Plant your feet on either side of the gate framework, grasp
with both hands low down on the metal edge near you and then
heave upward and drag sideways all at once. As you move,
shuffle your feet rapidly to keep pace with the gate. You look a
little like a pitiful Egyptian toting a rock up a pyramid.

As your man drives through the aperture, don't look at him.
Study the scenery, the sides of the road, or your bleeding
stigmata. If you don't catch his eye, and take your time closing
the gate, perhaps he'll refrain from that comment about the
width and swing of your backside.

Gate Type B: Those standard barbed wire and peeled pole
outfits. A barbed wire gate consists of three strands of barbed
wire stretched tautly between three upright wooden vertical
peeled poles. The first and third verticals are known as
"sticks", while the middle one is called a "stay".

Two general styles pertain here as well. The first kind stand
glistening in the sunlight. The new peeled-pole sticks glow
softly. The tight stretched barbed wire practically hums a tune
of pride in its own functional beauty. A wire gate is fastened by
a circle of smooth wire attached to the solid set-in gatepost,
then looped around the top and bottom of the first gatestick.
The bottom wire loop serves as an anchor and stabilizer. The
middle stave supports the three strands of wire as they pass on

---

* It is not necessary actually to spit, especially if you're not good at it. Just the
gesture will do. It's because you have observed your husband and the hired
hand doing it before tackling heavy jobs. Remember, you don't have to
understand why in order to have faith.

to the third gatestick which is anchored with wire to the other solid gatepost. Your job is merely to lift off the wire loop from the top of the first gatestick.

Wire gates have driven many a fledgling Eastern rancher back to the safety of the big cities. No self-respecting gate can be opened merely by lifting the loop off the top of the stick. In fact, no gate your husband has built can be opened at all except by a crowbar or your husband.* (see footnote) You, of course, are expected to pinch-hit for a crowbar. The secret is in the use of the shoulder. It's best to be wearing a jacket, preferably old, and already snagged. Snag damage reaches 87% among gate-opening Ranch Women.** (see footnote)

Approach the gate firmly. To cringe is to be defeated. Face the solid gatepost. Slip one arm under the top wire looped around the first gatestick. Reach across and clasp the gatepost in a bear hug. You will now be hugging and squeezing the gatestick and gate post as though you've found a long lost war hero. Grit your teeth, squint your eyes, grunt like the karate folks do, and pull mightily with your clasped hands while pushing like a draft horse with your shoulder. With any luck, the gatestick will ease forward enough to let you slip the wire off the top of the stick. WARNING: Sometimes a recoil from the release of tension can occur. Unsightly bruises to the face and body can result from nestling close to whiplashing gate sticks.

Now that you have the thing open, the easy part is over. Next grasp the loop-freed gatestick firmly, put your foot on the bottom loop and pull up, thereby unseating the stick from the wire loop at the bottom. Drag the entire gate either forward or backward. Of course, when you undo the wire loop from the stick, the three sticks and the wire which have been held tautly apart, immediately collapse in a battlefield mixture. So try to keep the three gatesticks reasonably tight and aligned as you swing open. Wave husband through the Appian Way. Again

* There are two reasons for tight-beyond-reason gates: one is to keep you alert and strong; the other is to discourage trespassers.

** The other 13% flat refuse to open gates or are 8 and 3/4 months pregnant or crippled.

avoid looking directly at him. Stare at the tires. Mention one is
low. Then while he steps out to look, you must slip the loop
back onto the gate stick. For some reason two more inches of
space now exist between loop and stick.

Don't cry out and don't admit defeat. After inserting the
bottom of the stick into the bottom wire loop, assume the same
hugging stance. Squeeze mightily. Scream once, softly. You
have caught a hunk of your shoulder between the wire and
stick.* (see footnote) Squeeze again. Take the fence stick out
of the bottom loop and stretch out the gate to try to yank out
the wrinkles. Insert stick bottom in bottom wire loop once
more. Assume correct gate stance. Squeeze. Close your eyes.
Grunt. Pull. Grit teeth. At that moment, over your shoulder, a
voice will rumble, "Need some help?" Instantly drop the entire
gate. Turn on your heel. Enter your side of the pickup and
quickly stop the bleeding and bind up the places where your
arm has been skewered.

If your husband remarks that the gate is a "little tight for
you," immediately assure him, "Oh, I could have closed it in
just a minute more," and change the subject.

Some wire gates are made even more super tight by the
addition of a "cheater", which is merely a stout stick, often an
old hardwood wagon spoke or a hame from an old horse
harness. The cheater is attached to the gatepost by a short
length of chain, cable or extra heavy wire. The chain attaches
at the gatepost and then to the cheater about one third along
its length. This engineering marvel utilizes leverage to aid in
gate opening. All you have to do is poke the short end (the one
third portion) of the cheater around the gatestick. The longer
end is then pushed hard causing a winching action which
squeezes gatepost and gatestick together allowing you to slip
off the loop from the top of the gatestick. The only drawback
to a gate cheater is that whereas it operates beautifully upon
gate opening, somehow on the return trip the distance is twice
as long. You can't get the end of the cheater stick anywhere
near enough to lever around the gatestick. There you stand,

* Most Ranch Women wear blouses with some sleeve, even in summer. This is
to cover the ugly purple marks left from viscious gates.

trying to force two polarized sticks towards each other. Only now you have one more stick thing in your hands to sort out. The thinking Ranch Woman will have her own cheater stick stashed somewhere out of sight. Behind the seat of the pickup is good. Paint your personal stick pink. Your husband isn't so apt to throw it away if it's pink. If he questions you, mention something vague about a craft project you're working on. Wind around your stick a good amount of all purpose baling wire. Thus you can be prepared for any gate. It is recommended that personal cheater sticks be employed only when you're alone. If your man is along, go into feminine flap and he will come to your rescue. It is on those lonesome forays to the South 40 when you can't get the gate shut and will be killed if you dare go on and leave it open that your pink cheater stick becomes a life saver.

The second style of wire gate is a great deal similar to the first style in basic construction. But instead of being super tight and impossible to open, these have broken sticks and/or broken middle staves held in suspension by the rusty wire clinging to them. Although there is no special muscle prowess needed to open these antiques, closing them can become a new dance step. Loose wire reaches barbed tentacles to entrap and ensnare. It's best to keep the whole mess pulled full length as you open and close. Keeping a tight pull is sometimes necessary to prevent the equally shaky fence from collapsing.

Type B gates include those big heavy wooden corral gates in a variety of sizes. They are very functional and very heavy which is perhaps why they always sag. The fastener is a wooden bar which shoves into slots in the gate post. As the gate sags, the slot stays where it is while the bar moves downward with the tired gate. Corral closures such as these cause hysteria in a Ranch Woman and evoke berserk rages from your ranch man because you don't get them shut or open fast enough. Naturally it's your fault if a stampeding critter gets away.

Before really severe sag-itis sets in, you can usually manage by lifting firmly on the gate while pulling back on the bar. As time marches on, the gate drops more. Eventually, there are about two thousand pounds of weight which must now be heaved upward each time you attempt an opening.

About then, the time arrives when it's your job to swing open the gate for an advancing group of heifers being shagged into the corral by your horseback husband. As the cattle close in, move smoothly to your appointed task. Except you can't budge the gate. Closer and closer come the critters. Frantically, you lift, heave and haul, but the only thing that moves is that slipped disc in your already damaged back. Finally, the heifers begin to scatter away from the gate.* (see footnote) Your man rides forward, swings off his steed, just like in the movies, makes several declarative statements using terse four letter words, jerks open the gate, remounts and rides off again to re-roundup the heifers.

At this point, turn on your heel, go to the house, march to the basement and fetch your very own chain saw. Stalk back to the corrals, kneel down, start the saw, rise and commence cutting a new slot below the old one in the gatepost. Pay no attention to what's happening in the corral, and under no circumstances speak to anybody or open any gates until you are satisfied you can.

* Cattle tend to react with terror at the sight of a medium size, plumpish woman moaning at the gate.

SECTION TWENTY-FOUR: HUNTING SEASON

Wherein one learns how to cope with those odd creatures—hunters. One learns what to tell them and what not to tell them. One also learns the correct method for helping husband butcher game meat.

In the fall along with nature's glory, come the HUNTERS. When the leaves turn gloriously golden and the deer from brown to gray, you know it's fall. You also know HUNTERS are on the way.

A primitive something strikes deep into the hearts of male persons—especially male city persons. Many and marvelous are the variations and combinations of hunter vehicles. Pickups with campers pull trailers; mobile homes pull jeeps; jeeps pull snowmobiles; converted school buses with flowered curtains at the windows pull horsetrailers. Some remarkable outfits manage to combine all in one wonderful conglomeration of wheeled motorized expensive extravaganza.

The interiors of the remarkable conveyances are equipped to the eyeteeth with all manner of hunter appurtenances, such as guns, knives, booze, a vast array of checkered shirts, electric socks, orange hunting vests, booze, jackets with special ammunition pockets, special ropes for the tying on of game, booze, red and orange plaid hunting caps and booze. On some mornings during hunting season, it's possible to hear a hollow thwacking that sounds like someone hitting a rotten log. Actually it's the echo of manly chests being thumped as armies of HUNTERS prepare to go after fierce wild meat.

City hunters spend a good deal of their time wandering up and down country back roads, searching for a PLACE TO HUNT. Most of the road wanderers stop and ask permission. Usually they rap on the door about five or six a.m. Sunday morning. (They don't hesitate to bang on your door at that hour because they've heard all farmers positively rise before dawn.) At whatever hour they appear on your stoop, you and your husband have a set of prepared remarks.

However, try to be kind the morning you are trudging across the barnyard and look up to see a remarkable apparition. A club cab pickup with camper pulling a small elegant house trailer behind itself is tippy-toeing up your lane. Hitched to the housetrailer is a miniature two-wheeled trailer upon which rides matching snowmobiles. Atop the camper, perched like a cap on a schoolboy, clings an upside down canoe. Clamped to the rear of the pickup sits a wire-spoke tote-gote, winking in the early rays of the sun. The assemblage stops when it sees you.

You stop also. You expect at least Pancho Villa, but what emerges is a mild looking, slightly paunchy individual who appears distinctly nervous. Since you carry nothing more intimidating than a grain bucket in one hand and three eggs in the other, and are followed by three peace loving dogs, a cat, a buckskin mare and two medium size sows, you are sure it can't be yourself making the man edgy.

It turns out he wants to know if the timber brakes along the creek bottom is "a wilderness area". It so happens that's the very pasture into which your husband has placed the weaned calves.

Instruct the man to come back later when your husband will be home. Mention he's not expected in until dark, because he's tracking down three rabid coyotes that have been ripping up the countryside. Or tell him the game is all in the high country and give him the name and phone of a local guide. Or whip out a map of the local Forestry Reserve Land and point out the "real wilderness" where crowds of deer abound. Lastly, offer to sell him a steer calf and promise to throw in a set of antlers from your son's antler collection.

Local farmers and ranchers who live in the country all year round do not take as many pains with hunting. When your husband goes after winter meat, he dons his cap with the earflaps, checks out his 30-30, drives to the upper section, quietly stalks downwind from a herd of grazing deer or antelope and picks off a buck. Usually he's back in two hours.

As a good Ranch Wife, you needn't feel left out on any possible glory. As soon as the mighty hunter returns with his kill, immediately leap into the role of helpmate.

Your spouse hangs the creature from a rafter in the old smoke house. After which he skins it. While he's skinning and removing the head and other unneeded parts, you are busy in the kitchen spreading the table with a piece of plyboard, finding the meatsaw, butcher knives and freezer wrap. Dissecting the animal is a necessary job especially if you want it to fit into the freezer. A competent meat cutter can whack up a critter into steaks, roasts, and chops in a short time. You are not good at all. In fact, the whole process is messy, bloody and very tiring. Therefore, it's best if you do not become proficient—ever. But certain steps may be taken to help maintain your image as a Ranch Woman. Wear a long canvas or rubber butcher apron or an old shirt of your spouse's. If you don't like the gucky parts of the meat, wear rubber gloves. Have two large waxed paper lined cardboard boxes ready for meat scraps. Place pieces of cheese cloth and string over the back of a nearby chair. As your husband cuts away the suet, wrap and tie it in pieces of cheesecloth. Later, hang them in the apple trees for the birds.

During your preliminary preparations, glance out the window from time to time. As soon as you observe your man heading for the house with a quarter of a deer over each shoulder, turn on the television loud enough to hear it in the kitchen. Next, make yourself and your man a tall spiritual beverage.

As the cutting chore progresses, keep freshening the beverages. Your man will be working so hard sawing through bones and chopping away the hard parts, he will sweat out any alcoholic effects. Since you are only wrapping the portions and marking the contents with a felt marker, you may develop a more severe reaction. By the end of a long meat cutting session, you should be so comfortable, all the blood and gore won't bother a bit.

If you are not a squeamish meat cutter, you are a True Blue Ranch Woman. You know neighboring ranch women who have no qualms and happily butcher all the ranch meat animals—steers, sheep, pigs or game. But remember, not everyone can qualify for Best All Around Ranch Woman Award. Somebody has to be among the runner-up group. Anyway, it's a lot bigger club.

PART FOUR:

WINTER

WINTER: That time of year when one huddles a lot. Mornings are a misery if your sheepskin slippers have disappeared. And if the pipes have frozen in the night, that trip to the outhouse is pure agony.

SECTION TWENTY-FIVE: FEEDING THE CRITTERS

Wherein one learns to drive the tractor or the pickup at snail's pace while your man throws bales to the cattle. One also learns how to throw the bales when husband throws his back out again.

Sometimes fall and Indian summer last clear until Christmas. More often the blizzards strike early. A crisp brilliant clear sky begins to cloud up. The air grays and thickens, and before long, that thick air congeals into gorgeous snow. The thing about snow is that it's everywhere and all over. Not a twig escapes the cold white blanket. While you may gaze in awe at the incredible beauty God has wrought over roof tops and fence posts, your man is apt to use the Deity's name in vain.

Snow and cold mean the cattle must be fed hay. The very hay you personally helped stack must now be dispensed, a few bales at a time, to the hungry critters.

Your man prefers to feed at daylight (naturally), which means you are required to rise in the middle of the night in order to feed him first. Also, naturally, you are privileged to help with the chore.

Gauge the layers of your outdoor attire by the outdoor temperature. The colder it is, the more sweaters, vests and warm socks you must don. CAUTION: Avoid squashing yourself too tightly into a many-layered outfit. The circulation can be squeezed from a limb in no time. The pain, when the blood finally begins circulating again, is excruciating.

When feeding in very cold weather, the following toilette procedure is recommended: Circle that long red woolen muffler around your neck, and up over the hood of your old red snowsuit. (Dudes from the city call a snowsuit a "snowmobile suit".) Wear your husband's o.d vest under the snowsuit and his old denim jacket over the outside. As mentioned, the trick is to avoid tourniqueting any part of your body. On your feet, wear the usual high-laced Penneys' boy's boots over two pairs of thick socks. Lastly slip on large four-buckle overshoes and buckle the tops over the pants legs. You will look like a displaced pudgy Eskimo. Try to avoid looking in a mirror or having to use the bathroom while thus outfitted. Lastly, feel your pocket to be sure you have your pocket knife, take up your warm fleece-lined gloves or mittens and stagger outdoors. When King-the-Collie rears up to greet you, make sure you are standing near a wall. Being bowled over in the snow on a cold dark morning is only funny in books.

Your man has not been idle. While you have been garbing* (see footnote), he has already loaded the pickup or the tractor's flatbed trailer with bales of hay. Whether you use the pickup or the tractor to feed depends on which pasture you're going to, and how deep the snow lies. As a good Ranch Woman, your job is to drive the vehicle while your man rides behind to throw off the bales. He will designate where he wants you to drive by waving his arms and pointing—similar to the way sheep dogs are directed to maneuver after sheep. You must keep one eye backward to watch your husband's signals,** (see footnote) and one eye forward to avoid falling in the irrigation ditch, sinking into a drift, or hitting a cow. Never go too fast. A lurching crawl, like a gluey-footed centipede, is the idea.

If you are driving the pickup, your man will yell "put it in the hole!" This means you are being ordered to utilize the very lowest gear—often called compound.*** (see footnote)

The tractor also has an extremely low gear whose location you can't remember. Unless you get really stuck though, a tractor can putz along as slowly as you wish even in higher gear.

Eventually, your man will drop the last bale and signal you to head for home. It is at this point many Ranch Women lose face. As you shift from compound, do not jerk. Otherwise, you may lose a good man off the tailgate. If you notice he's missing, be sure to stop and pick him up. He'll be a lot madder

* No one knows why it takes a woman three times as long to put on her outdoor gear, than it does a man. Try to get a head start dressing so you won't be left having to walk to the haystack again.

** When you can't see the signals due to the height of the load, you must hang one ear out the window and try to interpret the shouts. Attempts to use ESP do not work.

*** It doesn't matter what it is called. The important thing is to be aware that when "in the hole", the outfit will inch along over rocks, logs, and up the side of a tree if pointed to it.

124

if he has to walk all the way home.

There are those cruel mornings when it's entirely up to you to throw the bales because your man has put his back out. But he can still drive, although painfully. Ask him to back the outfit smack up against the haystack, then grab a bale hook and climb to the top of the stack. Many ranch men disdain bale hooks as nuisances when loading a haywagon. Pay no attention. Bale hooks are a boon and a pleasure to the Ranch Woman. The hook bites satisfyingly deep into the bale. You won't have to wear out fingers and wrench shoulder sockets trying to hang on to those bales by the strings. With a hook, you can drag a bale forward and then lift and heave. Be sure to unhook before you heave, otherwise the hook stays lodged in the bale and follows it down to the haywagon. Worse yet, you may still be hanging on to the bale hook handle.* (see footnote)

When the hay load reaches the proper limit,** (see footnote) jump on top and hang on while your man hurtles the vehicle forward to the feed ground. As he puts the outfit into its slow crawl, grab a bale by one of its two strings, give a mighty upward wrench while kneeing the center of the bale at the same time. Theoretically, the bale string will pop off like a rubber band. Then holding the one length of string, reach down and grab the other string, still around the bale. A quick flip and the bale flops apart and scatters over the edge of the wagon bed. Repeat this with additional bales at regular intervals, first on one side of the outfit, then the other. Each time after dropping a bale, you will be holding two strings which you then loop over a handy upright pole on the pickup. Later, you will burn the strings.

Unfortunate truth: The theoretically correct method of bale throwing only works some of the time. More often, the blame things fight back. Bales strings refuse to pop off no matter how hard you pull. If that happens, slip off your mittens and hold them in your teeth or stuff them in your back pocket, if you don't care for the slobber. Dredge out your pocket knife and

* At this point, your man's sense of humor asserts itself. He laughs himself silly.

** Try to keep mouth shut when your man comments on the flotsam and jetsam appearance of your load.

cut those reluctant bale strings.

Some sort of implement for cutting strings is a must. A tooth from a mower nailed to a stout stick works very well. Hold the tool aloft and bring it sharply down slicing the strings like a guillotine. An old hunting knife is the choice for some. Stick it, point down, in that skinny pocket half-way down the right leg of your snow suit. When needed, you can whip it out and whack the strings apart. (This particular method has a certain Wild West style to it.)

Sometimes, a string will break as you reach for it, scattering hay all over the load, but not onto the ground. Or you fall down, lose the whole bale over the edge with strings still tied and are forced to holler for your man to halt. Then jump down, run back, and break that bale. Tear back to the outfit and haul yourself aboard which is terribly hard to do in all those clothes, especially as the vehicle always starts forward just before you really arrive.

Finally you finish the job. As your man turns towards home, remain standing on the truck or tractor bed. Clutch firmly, anything available. Do not make the mistake of seating yourself on a bare board floor when returning from the feed ground. To do so will invite painful, long-lasting bruises as your husband guns the vehicle over the terrain, each wheel hitting a different frozen pie.

As soon as you reach the house, dash to the telephone and call the bone doctor. Plead mightily for an immediate appointment to have your husband's back overhauled, because your own is rapidly fusing into a permanent L shape.

SECTION TWENTY-SIX:
PROPER WINTER CLOTHING

Wherein one learns how the layered look in achieved for different temperatures.

Unless you farm or ranch in a warm zone, several months of the year must be devoted to the application of outdoor clothing to bodies. It is the ranch woman's obligation to keep track of jackets, boots, gloves, earmuffs, scarves, mittens, stocking caps, long underwear and fleece-lined winter caps with ear flaps.

In the big white house owned by Mrs. Super Rancher, the ideal storage organizer of winter wraps is a roomy group of closets and cupboards painted sparkling white, which never gets dirty or muddy. Inside, all jackets and coats are required to hang neatly on hangers. Overshoes and snowboots line up super neatly in personal grottos of a built-in polished redwood shelf unit. A clever drawer section of the redwood unit houses mittens, gloves and scarves.

Your own system may not be quite as perfect. Two long, paint chipped boards extend the length of one wall on the enclosed back porch. One board is above your head. The other is about kid high. Marching across the boards are hooks, and when those run out, giant nails. Jackets, coats, slickers, chaps, and irrigating boots hang there, like bunchy growths of some weird plant form. Beneath the forest of apparel is a long wooden box that once had a motor shipped in it. Rubber boots, four-buckle overshoes, snowboots, riding boots, one irrigating boot and two pairs of old holey tennis shoes spill over the edge. Mittens, gloves, scarves and stocking caps are supposed to be kept in two of the three drawers of an old commode. (The third drawer won't open and has no bottom anyway.) However, all the items as they are used, are piled on top. There's an unwritten law which prevents putting away any of these things. Eventually, there's nothing left inside the drawers, except for three left-handed mittens. Everything else is piled in a mountainous heap on top. Glove and mitten hunts can become a tradition with its own rituals. There are stirrers, pilers and scoopers. Stirrers slosh everything in a circle til they see something they like. Pilers stack everything like a hero sandwich and then try to find the perfect match. Scoopers merely scoop up a loose heap of gloves and mittens and let them rain down. Eventually they fish out two more or less equal mates.

Basic cold weather clothing begins in the fall with a light jacket over ordinary clothes. Progressively, additions will be made til the really cold weather clothing will include long underwear, warm shirt, sweatshirt, vest, snowsuit or coveralls and top jacket—lined. At least two pair of wool socks are worn on the feet, inside the high-laced boots. Four-buckle overshoes are last. In zero to 50 below cold, you can put a pair or two of your husband's big olive-drab work socks over the high-laced boots and then add the four buckles.

The last item, although not technically clothing, is truly of utmost importance. Throughout the pockets in the layers of clothing, stuff gobs of Kleenex. It is gruesome to be a mile from home with a continuously runny nose. Your **husband's suggestion about using a finger alongside a nostril should be ignored. You'll just get it all over you and make your sinuses hurt.**

With each additional layer of clothing, your agility is somewhat decreased. Finally you must be cautious or you will fall and roll away somewhere.

Husbands resist winter clothing. It has to be at least zero before a ranch man will admit his ears are cold. Although he will usually add a vest under, and a light jacket over, his unlined coveralls, his neck remains naked to the elements all winter. Whereas you are swathed to the eyebrows and beyond. In the very coldest winter, a ski mask with slits for mouth and eyes is excellent. If the wind is also blowing, add earmuffs.

During the winter months, be increasingly cautious when walking about, especially when feeding in the corrals and pig pens. When it's cold, all those fresh piles (and there are frequent new ones) tend to freeze immediately. Therefore, you must develop an adaptive gait. Lift your overshoed foot straight up, then forward and down—like the moon-walkers do. Should you get careless and walk normally, your forward moving foot will thonk into a frozen pig pile. The best that happens is a jarring impact followed by an irresistible forward leaning hippity-hopping momentum til you can catch your balance. Too often though, the impact crashes you to the ground. The grain buckets you are, of course, carrying, upend themselves or slam you painfully, or both. It's all right and probably therapeutic to curse and scream, but it's best not to linger there moaning. In spite of the pain, rise immediately, or you will have several swine trampling up your spine.

SECTION TWENTY-SEVEN: GETTING READY
AND SET FOR THANKSGIVING AND
CHRISTMAS FOOD CONSUMPTION

Wherein one learns to be grateful for all that stuff one canned and froze. One also learns how to shortcut and come out smelling like a gourmet.

The calves have been sold, the weaner pigs have been sold, the land payment has been made and the human offspring are settled into the routine of school. The weather has held nicely. Really foul storms have not yet descended. Number one son has actually done his homework several times without being reminded. Grab all the bits of peace while you can because the Holidays are coming.

The Good Ranch Woman is required to bake, cook and create vast amounts of foods forever. It's a bad mark on your Ranch Woman's Merit Page if you go out to a restaurant for a Holiday dinner or have anything catered or patronize a delicatessen. Since the last two aren't available in the country anyway, you have only the first item as an alternate choice to cooking. Even that may be taken from you since restaurants in country towns are apt to close during holidays.

Organization and stamina are the keys to success. During this season of the year, try to avoid colds and flu. Even if you catch something, you are not allowed to take time out to be sick. Over the years, a thinking Ranch Woman will evolve an attack plan to cope with Holidays. Some women develop a serious lassitude and have to be sent to a rest camp in Arizona. However, you are not financially prepared for that. And since the family won't pay attention to your symptoms anyway, you may as well roll up your sleeves.

Begin by dividing the work and activities into manageable segments. Segment one is food. You will need Thanksgiving food, Christmas food, New Year's food, and fancy tidbits for drop-in company, such as cute cookies and little stuffed pastry things.

First, pick a week around the middle of November. On day one, descend to the basement or tromp out to the rootcellar taking along a big basket or box. Fill it with an assortment of canned fruits, (especially apples), vegetables, and anything pickled. Back in the kitchen, search out the grinder, the chopping board, and the bread board. Have plenty of flour and sugar on hand.

In the freezer you have turkey, chicken and roasts you've been saving back. These present no problem besides drudgery. It's on the wide variety of fattening foods you must concentrate. Prepare a basic group of fancy breads, cakes and cookies. Think in terms of six batches of everything.

Stir up batter for six loaves each of two kinds of easy quick breads, such as carrot or applesauce. Add to each of these, raisins and smashed nuts. When the mixture tastes pretty good, pour it in loaf pans and stick in oven to bake. Always bake at a slow temperature. When still hot from the oven, pour on a lemon glaze. After the loaves cool, wrap individually in foil and freeze. That's one day's effort, and you are a little smug.

On day two, stir up a basic white cake and a basic spice-applesauce cake recipe. It's best to double these recipes three times. Trying to stir up a six-times batter won't work. You don't have a big enough bowl unless you use the canner tub which you might not be able to lift to pour out the batter. To each of the cake recipes, add a lot of raisins, currants, dried fruits and some of those mashed nuts. Then add a half cup of liquor—any kind. Bake in loaf pans (fill only half full) at moderate temperature for a long time. Just before you stuff them in the oven, arrange maraschino cherry halves in artful designs over the tops.

These "fruitcakes" can be frozen when done til you are ready for them. Or they may be wrapped in cheese-cloth soaked in booze and placed in airtight containers. Three pound coffee cans are good. When you think about it, moisten the cheesecloth from time to time with brandy or some other liquor. When the time comes, the fruitcakes can be served with a rum or brandy whipped cream. If you don't have the real rum or brandy, use vodka or gin with rum or brandy flavoring in it. No one can tell the difference. Be modest, but evasive when people exclaim over your superb fruitcakes and beg for the recipes. Mention (reverently) a Pioneer ancester who passed on the recipe with her dying breath while fighting off the hostiles. Baking the cakes along with all that tradition will have used up another day.

On the third day, stir up a big batch of yeast bread dough. Use buttermilk and several eggs in the batter. After the dough has raised and you are ready to work it, do anything except make plain old loaves. Work out a variety of shapes. Spread the surfaces liberally with butter, sprinkle generously with cinnamon, raisins, currants and some more of those nuts. Leave some plain and some with just celery seed sprinkled over. Then roll, twist, fold or sandwich the shapes together and automatically you have five or six kinds of dinner rolls. Arrange these in foil pans and freeze. When needed, put them on the heater to raise, then bake when ready. After baking, frost some with interesting colors of frosting for "sweetrolls". Making the rolls requires another day. By this time, you may find your enthusiasm waning.

Cookie baking and tidbit fixing could take up the rest of the week. You are a fortunate woman if you love to bake cookies and little candy things. In which case, leave this to last and best. However, if by this time you're sick of the whole business, it's time to cash those cream checks you've been saving. Then call the lovely Norwegian lady who does specialty baking as a hobby. Order six dozen of everything she makes. There is, however, no need to chatter on to anyone about this.

Merely mark off day four on your calendar. That afternoon sit down and read from two til four p.m.*

On the fifth day, devote yourself to making jellies. You have lots of canned berry juice in the root cellar. All year you saved and collected small jars of assorted shapes, especially "cute" ones. Baby food jars are excellent if you are going through that stage. (Somebody in the area will be!) Make as many different varieties of jelly as you have kinds of juice. Do one recipe batch from each type juice. (You'll have odd amounts of different flavors left over.) Fill the jars with the jelly and don't worry about more of one kind than another. Eventually you wind up with five or six varieties of teeny jars of

---

* Do not be tempted away from your reading program by housework or any emergency short of broken bones.

jelly. Seal with paraffin and mark the name of each on one of those Christmasy Santa or angel stickers and paste it on the appropriate jelly. Lastly, spray paint all the jar lids a bright color.

Jelly making day is a tough day, but when finished, you have all those containers of actual homemade jelly to give away to people who stop by at Christmas.* (see footnote) Package them in variety packs and send to city friends who have everything. Take some to the Woman's Club "bring a gift" Christmas program.

Combine all the leftover bits of juice mentioned previously into one pot. Using a standard cup of sugar to a cup of juice recipe, make a final big batch of jelly and pour into large jars for the family and label "Fruit Surprise".

On the sixth day of what has shaped up to be a very long week, make candy. Some women are candy making experts. They have secret recipes handed down by the original candy witch. These ladies go to marvelous lengths to produce creams, mints, bonbons and unnamed confections of all sorts. However, if candy making is not your bag, it works best to follow the recipe for fudge on the side of the cocoa box. Use real cream instead of milk and stir in a lot of extra butter and you can rarely miss. Think in terms of four. Make four batches of fudge, two plain and two with nuts. Prepare ahead several platters, plates and pie-pans heavily buttered and layered with rice crispies. Use two batches of fudge over the rice crispies. Spread the last two batches into plates or pans. Sprinkle the tops thickly with peanuts and/or coconut. (This is especially good for those people who like to pick nuts out of candy.) Always buy a jar of marachino cherry halves at Christmas. On some of the candy pieces, poke a half cherry for that professional touch.

If you feel you need another color of candy besides basic brown, make a penuche and do all the previously mentioned variations or make up some of your own.

An assortment of candy spread on a paper doily on a pseudo crystal serving dish looks terribly posh, especially if you add

* City people always remark, "You MADE these YOURSELF!? When did you find time?"

some of those Norwegian tidbits you ordered on day four. WARNING: Do not under any circumstances, leave unprotected a confectionary arrangement, especially if you're planning it for company. Children, cats, dogs and husbands become notoriously untrustworthy in the face of such temptation. It's best to hide the dish. Take care no one is watching when you stash the treasure.

On the seventh day—rest!

SECTION TWENTY-EIGHT: SURVIVING
THE ANNUAL CHRISTMAS PROGRAM
AT THE SCHOOLHOUSE.

Wherein one learns how to cope with the planned chaos of the annual school Christmas Program.

As Christmas draws nearer, you begin to feel you may be gaining on all the confusion. Then number one son mentions the school Christmas program again. What he failed to mention til now (the day before the event) is that he has a starring role in the Christmas play. This year, that pretty, enthusiastic new young teacher has the kids doing a skit about Sir Galahad and the Holy Grail. This particular bit was chosen mainly because the 8th grade has a preponderance of big boys this year. They're all making their own personal swords to wave about. What they're not making is the rest of the costume. Your son needs, he says, a knighthood suit. He also says all the other mothers have already made the other kids' suits. Jokingly you ask if he needs chain mail armour or will a simple knightly tunic do. He says he needs chain mail armour. Do not panic or hit him. Calmly pick up the wire basket and go gather eggs. To the chickens, express your opinions freely. They won't care, nor will they argue. Very possibly they will cluckingly suggest something helpful.

In any case, inspiration always strikes. Ask your son to don an old pair of jeans, an old work shirt and his old cracked riding boots. Have him wrap a towel around his head to more or less mask his face. Then spray him all over silver up to his neck. By the time you finish you'll both be giggling hysterically. Liberate some sheet tin from the shop. Cut two, ankle to knee, shingards and attach around his lower leg with thong. Then cut two tin half-moon shapes big enough to act like a short apron. One to hang in front and one to hang over the rear of your silver-hued son. The chain mail could have been a problem til you noticed the fireplace screen which just happens to be a flexible metal mesh. Borrow that. When circled around son's body and pushed up under the armpits, it hangs just above the tin aprons. Attach it by leather straps over the shoulders. Spray again. What to put on his head is a

puzzler til you recall your favorite rib-knit ski mask.
Mercifully you spray that silver before you put it on son's
head.* (see footnote) All in all, number one son makes a fine
looking Sir Galahad.

Number two son has been turning green with envy watching
his brother turn silver. Then teacher invites small son to learn
a poem to recite as the Opening Piece of the program.
Youngest son is torn between terror and a desire to emulate
his big brother.

The night of the performance is the usual planned chaos.
The two room, two teacher rural school bursts with Christmas
artistry created by the kids. In the largest room (about as big
as a double garage) incredibly hard benches and chairs fill all
the available free space in front of the homemade plyboard
stage. Seated on these torture racks are all the proud mothers
and fathers holding pre-schoolers on their laps. Aunts, uncles,
grandparents and neighbors swell the ranks. You are seated on
the aisle on the hardest bench halfway down the room where
you have a direct view of the stage.

At the side of the room stands an enormous Christmas tree
decorated with paper chains and foil things. On top, a giant,
smiling, paper-mache' angel leans precariously sideways. One
wing has come partly unglued and dangles upside down.
Folding chairs line up along the side wall before the
Christmas tree. Those persons seated there have to crane
around the foliage to see the stage.

As the curtain jerkily slides open on its safety pin rings,
number two son stands stage center, frowning horribly at the
audience. Hands jammed deep in the pockets of his brand
new pants, he rips off two lines of "Christmas comes but once
a year" . . . then goes into a decline. You sit aching with the
urge to help him, when a piercing whisper by the official
backstage prompter gets him going again. But not for long.
For the next nine out of the ten lines left, he has to be
prompted. Although he keeps his head rigidly facing the
audience, his eyes slip sideways at the end of each line. Then
they slide back for delivery. The last line about presents and
Christmas cheer he rips off with relieved finality. With no

* To make a knight requires three and a half cans of silver paint.

hesitation for any possible applause, he leaps forward off the stage, marches straight on past you, the proud mother all ready with sympathetic congratulations. Somehow his four year old determination parts the sea of people til he can clamber up beside his Dad who is seated on a table against the back wall.* (see footnote) Although Dad extends a congratulatory pat on the shouder, no words are exchanged, or necessary. The two men merely sit, duty done, right fists under chins, staring at the stage.

Recitations, songs and Christmasy skits follow the opening number. Number one son becomes a star that night. His knighthood suit is an outstanding success. He even clanks as he walks. Although he drops the Holy Grail once, he cleverly tips it upright with his sword. An eighth grade girl, playing a distressed maiden, develops a bloody nose but manages to keep her head tilted back so it doesn't drip on her dress. At a particular moment, the script calls for her to move near the edge of the stage—at which point a hand pokes forth holding a wad of saving tissue. Her remaining lines are delivered in a slightly muffled, nasal twang. At the end of the performance the entire cast receives a seated ovation.

After the final curtain draws together, an electric hearty "HO -HO -HO" reverberates around the room. In the back door lurches the standard fat-stomached whiskery Santa. From a giant gunny sack, he pulls individually packaged paper sacks of apples and candy. He passes out the goodies to the delighted children with accompanying clever, but not original, remarks. To the delight of everybody, Santa kisses the teachers and loudly recommends marriage between the single teacher and the only bachelor in the room. As soon as each child, including all the toddlers, has received a present from Santa, slip away to the back school room. You help spread out coffee, cookies, sandwiches and koolaide on the festively decorated table.

In a moment, all the audience begins to filter back to the refreshment table. Everybody stands around munching and talking. As the evening draws to a close, catch up with number

* All ranch men cluster like flies at the back and sides of any room filled with people.

one son and make sure he has all his armour collected. You'll need the fireplace screen.

Finally, the refreshment table is cleared by the mothers. The older boys collect the used paper plates and cups; the girls vacuum the floor and the teachers walk around slightly glassy-eyed. It's been an awfully long week directing all those child stars.

As the family drives home in a warm Christmasy glow, you remember that number one son will be home for two whole weeks to help his Dad feed the cattle! Gratefully extend warm congratulations on his performance one more time. Number two son is asleep on your lap.

SECTION TWENTY-NINE: WATCHING TV IN WINTER
(if you have TV)

Wherein one learns that vast numbers of women wear makeup, fancy dresses, and high heels EVERY BLESSED DAY. And wherein you wonder how those women would look wearing false eyelashes while feeding pigs in a blizzard.

The invention of television has been a blessing to all Ranch Women, especially in winter. Do not accept the notion you are being intellectually talked down to, or that your morals are being destroyed, or that your children will be seduced into violent anti-social behavior. Close association with farm animals exposes farm and ranch kids to a certain amount of sex and violence as a matter of course. The stuff on TV is often pallid by comparison.

For your husband, television is soothing relaxation and cheap entertainment after a day of battling the elements. Evening on a ranch is a wonderful time of day. It's usually short on conversation as your rancher man relaxes on the couch til unconsciousness arrives. BEWARE! Do not turn off that TV! To do so will waken husband who will claim he is watching. Do not bother to resent or take offense or feel in the slightest neglected when husband dissolves into sleep each evening. Be grateful. Remember, if he's asleep he's not pestering you while you're trying to catch up on your sewing or painting the woodwork or mending or a thousand other things. It is a basic law of nature that an idle man kept awake will pester. This takes the form of asking rhetorical questions or making comments on what YOU are doing. Or else he's teasing the dogs and cats or digging into the freezer for some more ice cream. Occasionally there are other interesting developments, but you can't always count on that.

For you as a Ranch Woman, TV has top priority on the list of household aids. In the evening it's company for you while your husband sleeps on the sofa. Those depressing monotonous jobs like overall patching and sock sorting can be made less screamingly boring with a TV set going. Also you can put in a lot of knitting time on Christmas presents for relatives.* (see footnote)

The primary and most important function of the electronic miracle of TV is the glimpse of other life styles. Even the word "lifestyle" came to you via TV. You didn't know you had one til you heard one of those commentators say so.

But now that you know about your lifestyle, it's up to you to take advantage of what you learn. Watch with interest the clothes the TV women wear and particularly observe what kinds of duties are involved in their careers and/or home life. As the young woman on the screen appears in daily costume change number three, you can ruminate about the rip in the paint-stained sweatshirt you've been wearing since yesterday. As you slip out of your high-laced work boots, note the panty-hosed legs of the TV model (male or female) demonstrating the toughness of hosiery fibers. Watch the model dash prettily up and down an airplane aisle as you meditate on whether you should put on that same pair of jeans again to slop the hogs. Note the velvet pantsuit the TV lady is wearing as a pre-luncheon outfit. Watch the TV woman's long slim tapered fingers with the polished shaped nails lift a stemmed glass. Glance at your own hands and note that the bandaide on your index finger where you rammed the barb wire into it needs changing.

It's OK to allow the influence of television to inspire you every so often to evolve a personal campaign of self improvement. First make a comparison study. Compare your livestock feeding garb with the elegant TV woman walking a dog. Her glimmering pale blue suit is topped with a short classic-line high-collared topcoat for proper winter walking. Down the city street she strolls, expensive kid gloves grasping a leather rhinestone embossed leash, on the end of which strains a small fluffy canine. The lady's face is a marvel of false eyelashes, blue eye liner and peach complexion, no doubt

* A hand knitted something wrapped around a jar of homemade jelly impresses city relatives who always ask, "Did you really make this yourself?"

achieved through the use of creams, potions and royal jelly.*
(see footnote)

Think about the woman in the see-through peignoir sip-
ping her morning mountain grown coffee as you don your
striped coveralls and raggedy denim jacket. Over your stubble
nailed fingers, draw yellow cotton work gloves three sizes too
big with a hole in each thumb, and think of Barbara Walters.
Arriving at the pig pens, shield your naked unmascaraed eyes
from the elements by pulling lower the brim of your old aviator
cap with the ear flaps. As you dump feed into a pig trough that
has no rhinestones, try not to giggle as you think of the lady
reading the label on the dogfood can through her riffle of false
eyelashes.

By all means try false eyelashes, but practice wearing them
long enough to strengthen your eyelid muscles. Otherwise the
lashes keep forcing your eyes closed making it difficult to see.
Such a handicap can lead to bruises and lacerations caused
from stumbling into objects.

Go ahead and wear the lashes as far as the pig sheds.
However, watch for gusts of wind which can catch you just as
you scoop the ground grain into the pig troughs. The granules
whip into your eyes causing lots of blinking and watering.
Don't forget the false lashes as you begin pulling at your upper
eyelid in order to blink out the grain dust. Otherwise you may
yank off a lash and then hastily attempt to poke it back. In
doing so you may ram a lash spear right into your cornea
causing terrible irritation and have to wear a black patch for a
week.** (see footnote)

As a true Ranch Woman you can spend a lot of time
laughing yourself silly over the hazards of trying to keep up
with the beauties on TV. The whole family is still talking about
the time somebody pasted a set of false eyelashes on Lily, the

* You tried royal jelly once. But since you couldn't afford $35.00 an ounce for
the stuff, you applied a bit of honey wax scraped off the top of the table honey.
After it dried, the muscles of your face did tighten up and presumably the wax
cleansed the pores. There was no doubt where you were all day. Everybody
merely looked for the cloud of flies.

** Your witty husband wittily offers you a Hathaway shirt to go with the
patch.

sow pig. To this day no one has admitted responsibility for "gilding the Lily".

Do not, however, despair. One day television will discover the Ranch Woman audience and slant programs accordingly. Soap commercials will spiel off slogans like "Ladies, you'll never complain again about excrement rings around the floor if you use new 'Gorp' " It's also a terrific restorative to aged ugly hands."

Hair spray ads will show a neat white-railed pig pen with a neat white denim trousered woman holding aloft a bottle of "Hold It Forever" hair spray. She bends and picks up a baby piglet. Her pretty locks bounce softly around her face as the piglet nuzzles her jugular vein. In a syrupy voice she compares the curl in her hair with the curl in the piglet's tail.

Other ads will feature a sexy young female beauty half naked, lying sideways on a pile of straw beckoning to a young male who is approaching, bulgy-eyed astride a tractor. She lisps, "Straw-Pile Perfume gets ME what I want!"

Future farm oriented soap commercials will portray a lady wearing a checkered gingham "farm" dress standing above her laundry pile. Over the dress she wears a folksy apron with a pocket that's never seen a smashed chicken egg. Gaily she looks into the camera and smilingly proclaims "one detergent— four settings—colors, whites, polyester and a special one for poop!" Then she holds up soiled coveralls stained with a brown substance simulating the real thing.

There are those time during storms when the TV aerial your husband has established on top of the pine tree on top of the hill, blows down. Then perhaps for days or weeks the ranch exists without advice from the outside world. But when the WORD returns to you, nothing is lost. The commercials are the same. The politicians are the same and the laundry instructions remain the same. Indubitably, the farm chores remain unsimulated.

SECTION THIRTY: WAITING FOR SPRING

Wherein one learns how to talk about hard winters, discuss how long the feed will hold out, and plan what to do to avoid winter doldrums.

As soon as the holidays have been met and conquered, the ranch enters into a period known as "waiting for spring". Waiting for spring includes that time from January second up to Easter. If the weather is fair to good, your man worries about shortage of moisture in the mountains and iminent terrible storms. If the weather dumps snow and cold over the land, he worries about blowing winds, drifting snow, shortage of feed, and the heifers who are due to calve in February.

"This is the worst it's been since the winter of '38!" says your man. Grunt your appreciation of this remarkable fact as you flip over a breakfast hotcake.

As a good Ranch Woman, appear to take serious interest in all weather talk, even though you've heard all the comparisons before. Weather is part of your daily routine. The kids go off to catch the school bus just before the weather report. Feeding the cattle and pigs occurs right after the weather report. Adjust layers of clothing according to the predictions. On mornings below zero or when a storm is predicted, send the kids off to school with their lunch packed in a double layer extra large grocery sack. In the bottom, pack extra mittens, muffler, sweater, and stocking cap. Sometimes the kids have to tote the giant lunch sack back and forth for several weeks, but a ranch kid is used to toting.

In January and February, TAXES drive farm and ranch operators berserk. The ranch boasts a businesslike hardbound, many columned record book into which is entered all the year's business transactions. But it's that giant calendar on the wall next to the telephone that serves as a daily diary. In case of fire, first grab the calendar, then look for the kids. Your husband never forgets to mark down a transaction. He records births, weights, sales, hay tonnage—everything but the egg money. (That's your job. And a nice lucrative bit of extra income it is, too.) Since the ranch pays for all the feed, you can keep all the income from egg sales as clear profit for yourself. Never reveal to the family exactly what you derive from egg sales. Ignore any person who attempts to point out that if the ranch is buying the feed, then you aren't REALLY making clear profit. Just go ahead and happily spend the money.

When TAX TIME arrives, a strange thing occurs. As it becomes necessary to cope with the incredible mountain of paperwork required to be allowed to continue existing one more year, your husband suddenly goes blind and develops a severe problem in his writing hand. He "lets" you "go ahead and do the books." He will, however, sign the forms.

During the waiting for spring months, you are likely to succumb to an affliction called obesity. To try to keep things cheery, it behooves you as a good Ranch Woman to bake plenty of cakes, pies, cookies, and especially doughnuts. For some reason, fresh doughnuts will cure the calving and blizzard blues faster than anything. After awhile it begins to look as if a doughnut the size of an inflated inner tube is attached around your middle. This is a problem for which no lasting solution has yet been devised.

While you and your spouse sit around, fatly watching the weather and eating doughnuts, mail order catalogs bloom. Surrounding himself with farm, ranch and machinery catalogs, your husband dreams of a new calf resuscitator of his very own. He leafs through page after page of tractor parts he must have. He diagrams new corrals he's going to build. He pores over catalogs advertising the Super Bull semen with which he plans to artificially inseminate his purebred heifers.

While your mate dreams through his wish books at one end of the kitchen table, you are immersed in your own fantasy world at the other.* (see footnote) Your magic pile consists of seed catalogs, household furniture catalogs, book lists and travel brochures.

In the seed catalog, make a check mark by everything you can possibly want. Then go back and put an X by those

---

* It's a country law that opening mail, kids doing homework, and catalog browsing are all done at the kitchen table regardless of any specially designated areas elsewhere.

practical things you absolutely need. Go through once more and place a circle next to the items that are on the borderline between absolute need and interesting experiment. Last of all, fill in the order blank with those choices that bear all three marks. Then match the total expenditures with what you think you can afford.

Since you are saving your egg money for extra special super interesting seeds, go out to the henhouse from time to time and add more vitamins and laying mash to the chickens' feed.

As you bite into still another doughnut, sort through the travel folders. Write letters to different agencies so they may advise you regarding group and family plans. They can't tell by the handwriting that you're a pudgy, doughnut-chomping, individual. Use flowery phrases and let them think you're one of the bikini Riviera crowd. One year an agency was actually going to send a representative, but it snowed and the authorities closed the pass for forty-eight hours, not to mention nobody got in or out of your lane for a week. But persevere. Travel planning is a harmless hobby and increases your knowledge of geography and history. Maybe next year the representative will actually get through and you'll make a new friend.

The household catalogs provide hours of fun and a modicum of heartbreak. Pick out a new couch to replace the broken spring monster in the living room. Remember, however, if it's a choice between a new couch and calf resuscitator, there is no choice.

If the creeks don't flood, the calves don't die, the market prices don't collapse, the grasshoppers don't eat the crops, the coyotes don't eat the lambs, a drought doesn't burn up the fields, and nobody gets sick, you may order brand new wall to wall carpeting for the living room to replace the beige colored tacky linoleum. In the meantime, do as all good Ranch Women do. Maintain a firm line that you PREFER linoleum on the floors because it's "easier to clean".

When you come to the book lists, go wild. Choose eveything that looks interesting. Pick out the craft and art and how-to books you love best. Then call your book-loving neighbors. Among you, work out a master list. With a little organization, it's possible to have access to a variety of books you've always wanted to own or read without putting up all the money yourself. Also, you get to read all the juicy X-rated books those OTHER women order.

In among taxes, calving and worrying about running out of feed for the cattle, the good Ranch Woman plans recreation and fun to relieve the winter doldrums for herself and family. During all the family fun outings, it's you who ride herd, keep track of gear and equipment and sort out time schedules. Once in awhile get away by yourself to indulge in a special secret desire.

Due to the rubber flab weighing you down around your formerly svelte middle, your pre-spring secret desire is to be thin. So you succumb to an advertisement touting a "Health Spa." The "Spa" offers ten sessions for practically no dollars. The initial evaluation and first lesson are absolutely free says the ad.

By some miracle, you manage to pack off kids and husband on an all day outing without you. Having made an appointment by postcard with the "Flower of Womanhood Health and Happiness Spa", you are free to partake. "The Flower of Womanhood Health and Happiness Spa" is a glittering building in the city. It has a lavender front and gold turrets. Try not to be intimidated. Go in.

Assume your best Ranch Woman "nonchalant air". Pause inside the door to absorb the atmosphere. Observe the lavender and pink reception desk decorated with gold leaves and gold turrets. Behind the desk is a lavender and pink and gold skinny lady. Effusively nice, the skinny lady, steps forward to greet you. She not only has a skinny body, but an elegant gold coiffure and pink fingernails. She wears a lovely lavender "doctor coat."

Courage! Put yourself in her pink lacquered hands. She is going to make you skinny, too! Try not to think about the gold and pink. Let her lead you and your frozen smile to the rear cubicle for a "weighing and measuring". Allow her to encircle your vast waist with her lavender tape measure. Share with her the slight shudder as she unbelievingly marks down the total on a pink score card.

After a series of interview questions, Ms. Lavender Lady dredges out your deepest secrets including the fact that your favorite sow's name is Peaches.

Lavender Lady leads you to "the course". Nothing makes you, as a Ranch Woman, more appreciative of ranch life than "the course". In a room the size of a horse corral, crouches an assortment of machines that move, grind, bump, massage, press, knead and whimper. Each machine is adaptable to a portion of you.

Do not falter. View the assemblage of leering machines as you would a bunch of pesky critters. Snub yourself into the one with the giant rubber band and allow it to shake the sin from your body for awhile. Next, seat yourself on the thing that resembles rows of giant ball bearings turning on a spool. As the top rows of bearings heave to the level of your seat, they knead your flabby person. When thoroughly kneaded, try the machine with a full length canvass belt. It looks like the drive belt on a tractor driven wood saw. Bravely lie down sideways and prop yourself on one elbow. Rhythmically, a padded hammer underneath the belt rotates on some sort of turning affair. The hammer mashes into the general vicinity of your waistline to "remove inches."

As the beat goes on, you begin to feel a strong yearning for home and family. Lying there like Cleopatra, note the other fat ladies draped around on the machinery. It's OK to smile in sympathy and offer a friendly word or two. However, try not to giggle. Remember, shedding excess lard is a grimly, depressing effort not to be tittered at.

Three hours and eighteen "Movieland", "True Love", and "Your Horoscope" magazines later,* (see footnote) you remove your body from the lavender machines. Smile brightly through the pain as you assure the Lavender Lady how wonderful you feel. Lie to her and solemnly state you will positively return next week. Maintain a thin posture as you exit.

---

* All salons and spas carry only these three categories of magazines. No one knows why.

Once in the car, relax your stomach and sit quietly for a moment. Rest your brow on the steering wheel if needed. Then drive to the "Jersey Lily Tearoom" and order a large chocolate-marshmallow ice cream frappe. Eat slowly while you read your book, "Fat Folks Have More Fun".

SECTION THIRTY-ONE: LAMBING

Wherein one learns what to do as a ewe midwife.

Stockgrowers still carry on the old west war between cattle and sheep. Some cattlemen claim they wouldn't have a*!''%$$(‡! sheep on the place because they stink, they ruin the grassland and cattle won't graze where sheep run! As a sheepwoman, pay no attention to any of that ancient controversy. Your small flock of woolies mix with the cows, the pigs, the turkeys and the chickens. No one told them they weren't supposed to live cooperatively, so they get along fine. The extra income from the lambs and wool provides an occasional new pair of shoes or curtains or even new heavy duty coveralls. Two years ago, when prices were good and coyotes weren't as plentiful, your lamb and wool crop purchased the new recliner chair that Blossom, the housecat, is so fond of.

Lambing season is planned for the end of April unless the bucks have gotten out and impregnated the ewes at a time unselected by you. In that case, you have to take the lambs as they come. As with pigs, cows, and heifers, the ranch personnel have to keep a round-the-clock watch on the lambing shed. You, as one of the high level personnel, have a prime responsibility. During lambing it's likely you may sleep in that recliner chair between trips to the sheepshed.

At some farms and ranches, the custom is to have the heavy wool sheared off the ewes previous to lambing. Others only "tag" the ewes and wait to shear after the lambs are born. (To "tag" is to shear only the wool covering the ewe's udders.)

The sheep shed or lambing shed is that long, low-roofed building far away on the other side of the cattle corrals next to the sheep meadow. Inside, two long rows of four by four wooden pens march the length of the building. Each with its own gate, the cubicles are called "jugs". The effect can be compared to a one level beehive or a one story condominium for sheep. Fresh straw covers the floor of each little apartment. Into the jugs go the brand new mothers and their lambs.

Some pens are larger, big enough to hold several mothers and children. After a day or so in a jug, a mother and baby can be turned into the larger pens with other pairs. A few more days and the new families are turned loose in the nearby meadows to graze. All these graduations help insure a lasting recognition and binding relationship between mothers and offspring. Otherwise, lambs and ewes tend to lose each other and bedlam ensues.

Every evening you and the kids bring the heavy ewes inside the shed where they run loose in the long open space not taken up by jugs. At 10:30 p.m., right after the news, garb yourself in your swell lambing outfit. A sheep person lambing costume differs very little from a pigging ensemble. Wear the standard striped coveralls over standard jeans and warm shirt. Don't forget your snaggedy denim jacket and the old aviator cap with the earflaps, especially during night forays. Even in April, ears can become awfully cold if they're left hanging out. Wear four-buckle overshoes because it's bound to be muddy. Carry your extra strong flashlight and trudge to the shed. Once there, walk quietly among the flock. Pick up the "drops"* (see footnote) and "jug" the new mothers and their lambs—which means pick up any newborn lambs and carry them into one of the small four by four pens. Hold the lamb low so mamma will follow along, baa-ing. Once the pair is jugged, go get the jar of iodine from the old refrigerator medicine cabinet standing in the corner. Lift up the new baby by the feet and slosh the end of the umbilical cord into the iodine. Usually mother is eager to help with the care of her lamb and gives no trouble. However, it's best to keep facing mamma while you handle her baby. Otherwise, you could find yourself butted off your dignity.

Sometimes a yearling ewe hates her offspring. Inexperienced, she is not quite sure what just dropped. But she is positive she wants no part of the thing. She sniffs, snorts, stamps her feet and leaps to get away from the horrifying little creature when it tries to nurse. It's your job to convince the young ewe that motherhood is her role in the rich pattern of life. If she has had her lamb in the open space of the shed, it's up to you to coerce her into a jug. First, pick up the lamb and

* Picking up a drop has nothing at all to do with nefarious doings, unlawful schemes, or manure.

jug him. Then try to discuss the situation with the yearling. She, of course, panics and runs to the other end of the shed. Move quietly among the flock and try to get the new mother up against a wall or into a corner. If she still spooks away, you may need to resort to a sheep hook, which is the original ten foot pole. The curved metal hook on its end, allows you to stand ten feet away and snag a sheep by a hind leg. Whichever method is used to capture the ewe, once you have her, grasp her firmly at the neck and quickly sling a leg over to straddle her, facing her head end. Hang on to her head with a hand on either side and start motivating towards a jug. If the ewe is large and you're short legged, you may find yourself in an unstable situation. In which case, if she hasn't already dumped you, get off her back. Grip her fiercely on the side of the head with one hand and grab on to her tail end with the other. Get a good tight squeeze hold and aim her for a jug. Once she takes off, you must pitter patter rapidly alongside to keep up. You look a little like one of the clown acts in a performing circus as you zip around the shed. Another method is to grab a hind leg and propel her like a wheelbarrow. This works fairly well unless she outweighs you..

Once you have the reluctant yearling jugged, encourage her to allow her new child to take nourishment. Establish firm control by holding the ewe still while junior searches. Unfortunately, the nuzzling of the baby lamb may drive her to frenzy. She rips out of your grasp and skitters frantically around the jug while junior bleats pitifully. In order to promote a more meaningful mother-child relationship, take a piece of baling twine and tie mother's back leg to the pen side. Having to stand on her remaining three legs insures she can't kick her child away when he tries to find his dinner. Another method is to employ your pocket knife and cut a gunny sack lengthwise into two strips like long bandages. Pass one strip behind her front legs and around her body and the other strip around her body in front of the udder. Tie each strip to the side of the pen. The length of time required for a young new mother to accept her lamb varies from a few hours to several days.

Sometimes a ewe has trouble delivering, particularly if it's her first born. If you observe a ewe in trouble, urge her into a jug. Then quietly grasp her around the neck in a hugging action. Lift her up so her front feet come off the ground and she sits back on her haunches, then gently ease her over on her side. Usually she'll remain quietly where you put her, but if not, straddle her and sit down facing her rear end. Perhaps the lamb's head is turned back or perhaps it's a breech presentation. Whatever the trouble, remove your gloves and insert your hand in the delivery aperture to ascertain the position of the forthcoming lamb. Adjust the head and legs to proper alignment. The front feet should slip out first with the nose resting on the forelegs. When the ewe next contracts, help her by pulling steadily on the baby feet. If all is well, out pops a lamb covered with a golden orange stuff. Make sure no membrane covers his nose, lift him up by the back feet and shake him to promote coughing out phlegm. Then work the lamb's front feet back and forth to help insure proper breathing. As soon as he's breathing well, iodine the navel and poke him under mamma's nose, (if she isn't already sniffing him) so she can get on with the job of licking off her baby. In just a little while, the lamb staggers to his feet, crowds into mother and begins to nurse.

Sometimes a ewe can't raise her children. Sheep are inclined to double and triple offspring. Since a ewe has only two teats, unless she's an exceptional milker, one of the lambs may become a "bum".

For whatever reason, each spring sees several bum lambs. Some big ranches give away the bums to anyone who wants the trouble of raising them. At your place, you and the kids get to have all that fun as substitute mammas.

Pen all the bum lambs together as they come along and start feeding them four times a day. Begin with a sixteen ounce pop bottle (fitted out with a nipple) half full of milk per feeding. As the lambs grow, they don't have to be fed as freqeuntly, but the amount increases to about two quarts of milk per day.

Feeding the bums requires a system. Your system is to assign both sons the responsibility. The boys learn all that self-sufficiency, plus earning themselves some income when they sell the lambs and wool. A small problem lies in the fact that so often the kids are in school and it's you who tramp to the lambing shed or the barn toting a mixed bag of bottles of milk. The instant you step over the portal, the lambs recognize you as Mom, and baa piteously. When feeding bums, you need eight hands. As you stuff a bottle into the first two faces, the rest bleat, blat, and hop around trying to crawl into your pocket. Watch that you don't accidentally feed a greedy woolly twice. If you have too many to keep straight, take along a giant magic marker or piece of colored chalk. When you are holding a bottle in each hand with a lamb attached, slurping away, it becomes difficult to reach in your pocket for that marker. Therefore, previous to stuffing the lamb's faces, stuff the end of the marker or chalk into your own mouth. Then bend your head down over each little angel as he eats from the bottles you hold and swipe him across his nose. This method works OK except you're apt to jab too hard and drop the marker or jam it sideways in your face. Besides, it tends to become slippery with saliva if you have a lot of bums to mark. Another method is the "knee catch". As soon as you have two lambs firmly established on a bottle each, place one bottle between your knees and grip it tightly. This frees one hand to reach in a pocket for the marker. Take care you do not attempt to walk while in the knee catch position or you will lose bottle and marker and become hopelessly confused.

As your little lamb family matures, they begin to follow you about the barnyard like a woolly parade, each one calling Ma-a-a-a!

PART FIVE:

WOMAN WORK AND WOMAN ACTIVITIES

"Woman Activity" includes all those community activities you do that you don't have time for but squeeze in anyhow. "Woman work" includes all those household duties and nasty maintenance chores, cleanup jobs, and eye-straining secretarial and bookkeeping tasks your man "lets" you do.

SECTION THIRTY-TWO: SLEEP

Wherein one learns that sleep is a forbidden luxury.

If you live in the country, sleep may be defined as that restful commodity you're not allowed in the mornings. Country custom says you must get up before dawn in order to be ready for the day when it begins. This is vital. If the rancher isn't up, the sun is unable to tell if it should rise and shine. Coping with any untoward happening, no matter how trivial, is accomplished in the country by getting up an hour earlier. A serious problem means rising in the middle of the night.

Among city people, a belief exists that all country folk automatically pop up in the pre-dawn with a glad heart and a light step. Not true. As in the city there are morning people and night people. However, in the country, regardless of your own physiological inner time clock, you are REQUIRED to be a morning person. It's a cruel world in the early hours for those country women who are NOT morning people. While husband rises to his greatest heights of oratory in the early morning, you can barely breathe. Your dearly beloved has learned to refrain from asking questions that require actual answers. He seems satisfied with nods, grunts and an occasional moan, which is the best you can manage.

Although no real help exists anywhere, night-person Ranch Women have collaborated to formulate the following sleep rules.

Rule 1: If you help with the milking, never volunteer for the morning shift. When your husband rattles the milk buckets on his way out to the barn, turn over in bed, place pillow over head, and grab a few more moments of sleep.

(Shameful Habit: failure of the Ranch Woman to leap up and prepare hot coffee for her ranch man.) (Comforting thought: nobody will hang you if you ignore that custom.)

How to get around shameful habit: (a) make a fresh pot of coffee the night before and leave it plugged in or (b) assemble a giant extension cord that runs from the kitchen, down the hall, around the corner and into your bedroom to fetch up at the wall plug on your side of the bed. Splice into the cord one of those on-off switches. The second the alarm screams in the morning, without even removing your head from under the covers, reach out and push the switch to "on" position. By the time your man finishes dressing and firing up the heater stove, the coffee will be fresh and hot to greet him. This entire system can be constructed for under five dollars depending on how far it is to the bedroom* (see footnote) When you hear the back door slam signifying the cow milker's return, crawl out of the nest, slide into some sort of clothes, and be standing in the kitchen holding a cup of coffee and a spatula to make it appear as though breakfast is practically ready.

Rule two: Establish one day (usually Sunday) as your personal and deserved sleep-in morning. Refuse to crawl out before at least 9:00 a.m. Do not succumb to the myth that the ranch will fly to bits without you on deck at 6:00 a.m.

Rule three: To insure non-disturbance for your chosen morning sleep orgy, stash away a batch of yummy sugared cinnamon rolls in some secret place. At bedtime the night before, (make sure everyone else is already sacked in), unearth your goodies and place in the center of the kitchen table under one of those cake-saver containers. On top, leave a note which may be reused each week. The note need not be poetic unless you are so inclined. The message directs early risers to eat all they wish QUIETLY, while warning of fatal disaster should any attempt be made to storm the sleep fortress before YOUR chosen hour.

Rule four: Should any of the preceding rules be infringed upon, do not kill in anger. Say nothing. But the following week, put out the cake box in the center of the table again. Inside the cake cover place a note that says "Surprise! No goodies today. Tune in again next week." (This note may also be saved for re-use.) The following Sunday, re-introduce the cinnamon rolls with the standard help yourself note. This method is NOT a can't fail prescription, but it works pretty well most of the time.

Early out of the nest in the mornings is such a sacred country custom that a ranch man would die before he'd be

* Do it yourself plans for the Ranch Woman Coffee-Pot-Switch-On-System can be sent on request. Clear diagrams included.

caught in bed after sun-up. So strong is this habit that ranchers who need to phone each other for business reasons always do so between five and six-thirty a.m. The stated reason is so the first rancher can catch the other "before he goes outside." At 5:30 a.m., in the pre-dawn when the phone screeches, your husband immediately leaps from betwixt the covers, grabs a shirt, staggers to the phone and bellers "HELLO"! Your rancher man immediately claims he is up to the caller; in fact, he says, he was just on his way to the milk barn. (Meanwhile he is shrugging into his shirt, his naked legs hanging out below, gathering goose bumps.) If he needs to call a neighbor, your spouse sets his alarm an hour early so he won't be late to call neighbor Sam, because "Old Sam gets up pretty early." You know darned well Old Sam also is standing there at his end of the line half naked and shivering. But do not offer any comment. Just press your coffee switch-on button and go back to sleep.

On a morning when your mate may feel justified in sleeping in, after perhaps being up with a critter half the night, he rises in the pre-dawn as usual, gets completely dressed, then lies down for a nap on the couch. First, however, he turns on a light in the kitchen so that any possible early passersby on the county road will know he's up and about.

SECTION THIRTY-THREE: COFFEE,
COOKIES AND DAILY MEALS

Wherein one learns that coffee and cookies are a country staple. One also learns country meal preparation and how to develop certain shortcuts for sanity's sake.

It is of prime importance NEVER to run out of coffee on the ranch. ALWAYS keep the pot hot. Country custom says gallons of the brew must be consumed daily. Farmers and ranchers have stomachs, livers and kidneys impervious to strong beverage. NEVER substitute tea, cocoa, or some other new-fangled city drink. Even if the ranch man really doesn't like coffee, he would rather turn down coffee than tea.

To go with the coffee, cookies are an absolute must. Always have the cookie jar full of HOMEMADE cookies, of course. If store boughts are substituted, profuse apologies must be offered. Make great batches ahead of time and store. Country custom says the good Ranch Wife always piles a plate high with cookies to offer guests along with coffee. Do not ask your guests if they want any. Repeat: do not offer a choice. Place the heaped plate in the middle of the kitchen table, around which everyone is, of course, sitting.

In the country, meals must be served at given hours promptly and constantly. Lots of food must be available at all times. Vast quantities of meat, bread and potatoes must appear three times a day. Twice a day, dessert is a requirement (and always cake or pie one of those times) to round off the meal. (Cookies not generally used as dessert, but maintained as filler for mid-morning or mid-afternoon coffee and/or drop-ins.) In summer, it is OK to add ice cream to the dessert menu. Preferably homemade and usually glopped on top of the cake or pie.

Breakfast starts with the usual gallons of coffee followed by several eggs, pancakes and/or hot cereal with fresh cream. If any potatoes are left from the night before, fry those also. Fruit juice is optional. If you want your ranch man to have his vitamins, place glass of juice or vitamin pills in front of him.

He will automatically drink and/or swallow pills..

The one redeeming feature of breakfast is the sameness of the menu. The routine is easy to learn. This allows you, after some practice, to make breakfast while still asleep on your feet. There are no other redeeming features.

No deviation is allowed concerning dinnertime which is ALWAYS at high noon. Prepare large joints of meat, many potatoes, kettles of gravy, salads, vegetables, gallons of coffee and, of course, dessert. Biscuits or hotbreads or homemade loaf bread is a rigid requirement. It is an absolute ranch law to have bread of some sort.* (see footnote)

WARNING! You may set the table and put the salad on, but NEVER NEVER place the meat and potatoes on the table until you yourself are ready to sit down. Otherwise you will find yourself eating alone. The ranch husband is not impolite; it's just that eating is a reflex and he can't resist the food if it's placed before him. An alternate plan is to remove all the kitchen chairs to a far corner or to another room, which makes it safe to put all the food on the table ahead of time. If these precautions are not observed, the rancher will wash up, sit down to the table and devour food. Some ranch husbands try to restrain themselves to wait for the woman to complete last minute tasks and sit down with him, but BEWARE! Even those superbly controlled fellows will scoop portions of food onto their plates, mash on their potatoes, pour their coffee and clutch knife and fork, to sit poised at the ready. The second you move to sit, he has you outdistanced, no matter how fast you chew.

The one redeeming feature of the meal is that there is no dawdling. Food is met, conquered and disposed of in record time. Conversation is limited to breathing between bites. When the final bite occurs, a last cup of coffee poured, and a toothpick arranged in the face—then the contented husband may, and probably will, talk.

Supper is slightly better in terms of preparation. As a good Ranch Wife, cook enough for the noon meal so that you can have leftovers. Or chop up everything and make soup. The

* Baking bread is extremely high on the list of Ranch Woman arts.

supper meal should be at 6:00 p.m. However, some flexibility is allowed here. You can be later without stopping the sun in its tracks, but not TOO late. The clever Ranch Wife mixes a toddy for her man AND herself, then fixes the supper while he sips companionably and talks. This is one of the warm spots of the day when your husband **likes** to talk. Really a pleasant time, spoiled only by the fact of one more meal to organize and clean up after.

SECTION THIRTY-FOUR: WASHING THE SEPARATOR

Wherein one learns basic attitudes towards the milk separator.

Dealing with a separator is a matter of constantly bearing a cross. A malevolent contraption of stainless steel, the separator consists of a big fat round bowl large enough to hold better than a milk bucket full of milk. The bowl lets the milk down through a valve opening where it enters a gismo that encases a series of metal discs layered closely together. When turned on, the casing full of discs whirls faster than the speed of light. The milk passes through these, and magically, the milk and cream flow into separate spouts that channel into separate containers. No one really knows how the machine can tell which spout leads to cream and which to milk. But it never errs. You, however, are not so perfect.

Washing the separator is a ghastly, hideously boring, cruel Albatross of a chore. One ALWAYS done by the woman. He milks—you wash. There is no way out. And there is no way to make the chore pleasant. But there are a couple of things to make it less boring. For instance, you can time how long it takes you. After a week, you will have shaved several minutes off your record. Or you can wash the monster only every other day. (But don't tell anybody and keep milk for yourself only on the alternate clean days.)

If you're not there to wash the separator, leaf by scummy individual leaf, the thing visciously mucks up its innards on purpose. Years of your life as a Ranch Woman are spent toiling over the evil-hearted beast. All previously refined Ranch Women learn unique curse words as they pick up and try to fit together all those accidentally dropped separator leaves.

If your rancher man is away for a day or two, and YOU get to do the milking, the separator job remains yours. If YOU are away for a day or so, your spouse does the milking, and the separator job remains yours. The crud simply continues to build until you get home.

A third and best alternative: get somebody else to wash the

cursed thing. Since that never happens, you are stuck forever and ever. There are no redeeming features to this chore, whatsoever.

Separator washing can, however, be employed as a strategic weapon. If any kid balks at garden weeding or wood hauling, suggest a trade in jobs. As an alternate to washing the separator, persons of any age or sex will do almost anything.

The only relief from year around separator washing is when one milk cow goes dry and the other hasn't come fresh yet. Actually, such a situation has occurred only twice in six years, so it is not a relief you can count on.

Different Ranch Women develop different personal techniques for separator washing. Ideally, it's best to have two giant built-in metal tub-sinks right next to the separator in the utility room just off the back porch. Above the sinks, stainless steel metal rods extend across from wall to wall forming an open grill work shelf. Upon this, place the dripping scalded separator parts as you interminably wash them. The big sinks can hold the entire pile of separator pieces or a whole milk bucket can be immersed.

Some separator washers prefer to charge right into the job first thing in the morning. Others, with weak stomachs and poor self discipline, are inclined to wait until the evening newscast or the Johnny Carson Show before tackling the thing.

Many, many country woman legends have accrued regarding correct separator washing techniques. Do not be intimidated. Ghosts of separator washers past will not rise up to strike you down in the dishwater if you change the rules.

Once the beast is washed and hung up to dry, the nasty portion of the chore is finished. The merely irritating part comes next. Previous to the next milking, the separator has to be put together again in a certain sequence. Each part is important and each part knows where it should go even if you don't. Get one disc out of line, forget the rubber ring, or fail to tighten the cream screw, and a veritable disaster follows. When foaming milk is poured into an improperly assembled separator, the liquid immediately spurts and cascades seven feet in seven directions. Should such a horrendous catastrophe occur, think fast. Close the valve and flip the switch to off! (It is optional to employ swear words you've noticed the men use in the corrals.) Then find a mop. While mopping, it's therapeutic to rehearse what you're going to say to anyone who chances upon you while sopping up the mess. It's OK to accuse the party of deliberate sabotage. Should that person have the gall to snicker at poor you, scathingly instruct him where he can put the separator AND the milk cows.

As a last ploy, silently hand the mop over and leave. For days afterwards, the utility room has an odor reminiscent of unhousebroken cats. Don't let this bother you. Place two or three incense burners at strategic spots to catch the cross drafts. Light different flavors of incense sticks as burnt offerings. Double the incense arsonal if Mrs. Super Rancher is expected.

SECTION THIRTY-FIVE: VISITORS

Wherein one learns the proper rituals, customs and etiquette when visiting or being visited. One learns certain techniques to divist oneself of visitors while remaining polite.

A ranch or farm may seem isolated to the casual city observer. Except when snowed in, however, there's really a lot of traffic flowing in and out the back door of any country dwelling. (In the country, front doors practically fossilize. In summer, the front door may be opened to obtain a cross breeze, but no one uses it to gain entrance!) Through the back door and into the kitchen arrive all visitors. These can be classified into two general types.

Type A is the neighboring rancher on an errand "stopping by" to see your husband. Instantly offer coffee whether you know the person or not. He will say "no thanks", and will then wait in his pickup for your man's return from the South 40. Or he will head out for the South 40 to find your spouse. In either case, if for some reason, the rancher's "woman" is along, she will have been left sitting in the pickup. Always look out the window to see if this is so. Tell the visitor to invite his wife in, or if he's wandered off after your husband to the South 40, go out to the pickup and invite her in yourself.

If your husband is home when the caller stops by, follow the same routine with slight variations. Place coffee and cookies in front of husband and caller. Instruct caller to invite wife in (you have already looked out window and observed woman in pickup). If caller says, "No thanks, I'll just be a minute," then you are obliged to go out to pickup and chat with the wife through the window. Do not put on a coat. Cross arms and shiver and chat. You do not introduce yourself and she does not introduce herself. If her husband does not emerge from the house shortly, re-invite her in. This time she will dismount and accompany you to the house where you place coffee and pass cookies. When the two husbands are finished talking business, say goodbye to the woman, always ending conversation with "stop by sometime." Saying goodbye to the husband is optional. As soon as the pickup pulls out of yard, ask your husband the wife's name. He will not know, but does know she milks eight cows by hand every day, without help.

Type B visitors are social callers. These usually come in packets of two, a man and wife. Occasionally there's a foursome. They usually have just "stopped by" and usually without phoning to see if you're home, ready for them, or have other engagements.

When you hear the vehicle enter the yard, and see who it is and become aware you're going to be VISITED, immediately dash for the bedroom and jerk up the covers on the unmade bed. Leap back to the kitchen. Wipe off table. Go to door carrying dishtowel. Smile broadly and joyfully.

When everyone is seated at the kitchen table, spread around the coffee cups and break out the cookies. Make some attempt to coax everyone to come sit in the living room. You may or may not be successful. Usually the men retire to the comfort of the living room armchairs, leaving the women hauling the coffee and cookies after them. Then the women return to sit on hard chairs in the kitchen, occasionally interrupting their chatter to pack in the coffee pot and refill the men's cups. Sometimes the order is reversed and the women sit in the living room, leaving the men in the kitchen. However, the women still see to it that the men's cups are kept filled.

Country custom says that men and women shall not sit in the same room and converse TOGETHER, especially if more than one other couple is present. If only one couple is visiting, women sometimes may sit in the same room with men, but are expected to converse with each other—not with the men.

When the situation is reversed and you do the visiting, follow the same customs. Visiting can also be classified into two general categories. Type A visiting includes accompanying your husband on an errand. At times, you "ride along" while your man "stops by" another ranch on a matter of business with the other rancher. You will be left sitting in the pickup, talking through window to the other arm-crossed shivering Ranch Wife because your husband will "just be a minute." Often, however, there is no wife present to talk with. Ranch men prefer to track each other down in unusual and generally removed places—like halfway down the irrigation ditch. For these lengthy moments, the wise Ranch Woman keeps a care package in the glove compartment of the pickup. Frequently a sanity saver, the package contains chewing gum, supplementary food, kleenex, comb, lipstick, and MOST important—a book or magazine to read during those "few minutes" of waiting.

Sometimes your man and the other rancher conduct their business through the pickup window. You still can manage to get in a lot of reading, as a great many moments will elapse between remarks, none of which will be directed to you anyway. Ten to fifteen minutes or a whole chapter pulsates by before the point of the visit slips into the conversation. The weather, the calves, the sheep, the neighbor's lame colt, the price of cattle and hogs, ditch cleaning, another neighbor's drunken hired hand—all these will be mentioned while the conversationalists gaze at the far horizon. In fact, the two men will say their goodbyes, your husband will start the pickup motor, you will close your book and ready your goodbye smile, when your man offhandedly inquires, "By the way . . . " At this point, you can get in another half chapter.

Always it is a pleasure to receive visitors and catch up on what's going on in the county. Sometimes, however, you may be driven to the point of rudeness when certain thoughtless visitors begin to camp underfoot while your lambs go unfed and the separator remains unwashed. There's always a family like Pudwell Buford and his brood of six kids who visit en masse. Pudwell and his wife, Luella, arrive at 8:15 in the morning and settle themselves in. Mr. Buford awaits your husband's return from the feed ground, he says. Luella just likes to "come along and visit." The kids, range in unwashed ages from two to thirteen. Pudwell believes that a family that visits together ought to.

To rid yourself of Pudwell Buford-type visitors, be bold. Country custom says you must not point to the door and order them out. Country custom also says if they're still around at meal time, you must feed them. Maintain cheer, pour coffee once around and put out a skimpy plate of cookies. When the cookies are gone and the coffee pot has gone dry, do not replenish. If it is summer, close all the doors and windows, put on a sweater and mention you have a chill. Then build a roaring fire in the cookstove. Cough a lot and sniffle some. When the Bufords make noises about leaving, give them a dozen eggs on the way out.

If it's wintertime when the Buford tribe comes a calling, do not falter. Open all the doors and windows to "air the rooms." You can wear something especially warm and stand over the cookstove. Let the coffee pot run dry and wait for their chilblains to rise. Give them a dozen eggs on the way out.

SECTION THIRTY-SIX: COPING WITH
THE ANNUAL 4-H FAIR

Wherein one learns to bear up nobly.

Each year the county sponsors a "4-H" Fair where kids can exhibit animals and display produce they've raised themselves. Boys and girls from seven through high school are eligible. To be a 4-H er, one strives for a head that is clear, hands that are useful, a heart that is kind, and health that is good. Crafts, needlework, sewing, woodworking and scrapbook projects dealing with farm and range management may also be submitted. Vegetables and crop plants are harvested at peak perfection and presented. Cookery, from biscuits to pies and cakes and even full meals are entered. Selected judges taste these offerings.* (see footnote)

For the parents of a 4-H child, the experience is not only inspiring, it's also a test of patience, agility, and mental balance. As a Ranch Kid's Mother, you automatically participate in 4-H activities, as chief honcho, herder, binder up of wounds, salver of hurt feelings and fierce protector of your own offspring.

Last year, first son entered his registered Hereford bull calf in the competition. He had purchased the calf with his own money. By Fair time, the little darling had grown to 800 pounds of stubborn muscle and bone. All spring and summer, "Colorado's Golden Boy" (the name listed on his papers) had been a constant companion to number one son, who for some reason decided to call the calf "Blister".

Early in life, Blister must be taught to lead. When you pass by the corral one morning and observe a calf galloping and bucking at the end of a halter rope, ask no questions.

At the other end is a person you recognize as your son, heels dug into the turf, body slanted backwards, grimacing ferociously while he hollers "Whoa!" and other words you didn't realize he ever employed. A determined lurch by the rambunctious calf jerks the 110-pound boy off his feet to land belly down, still hanging onto his end of the halter rope. Do

* Never volunteer to be a taster.

not panic. Quietly go on about your business. Nobody likes to be happened upon in such an inglorious position, especially by a relative.

But there are times when you are allowed to help educate Blister. "Setting Up" a calf is the art of showmanship. The calf must be taught to stand with legs squarely under him and head held alertly straight ahead. A long stick called a show stick is used in "setting up" the animal by tapping errant feet until he stands square. The stick is also used to scratch the calf's belly, which theoretically soothes the beast and keeps him calm. Blister loves to have his belly scratched. Or he does now. At first, while your son made repeated attempts to "set up" Blister, you were chief belly scratcher. Blister, however, failed often to realize he was enjoying himself and kicked the stick plumb out of your hand.

Blister must be bathed, combed, brushed, "blowed" and clipped. His horns must be sanded and oiled and his toenails trimmed. The whole family gathers to hold things while Number One Son "pretties up Blister". Garbed in a yellow rainslicker, and four-buckle overshoes, your son takes the hose and turns a stream of water onto the calf. Then a machine that looks like a vacuum cleaner is employed to blow and fluff him dry. As a matter of fact, the machine probably IS a vacuum cleaner—yours. After blowing and fluffing, number one son, aided by four and a half year old number two son, goes at Blister with brush and comb. At the front end, your husband gives advice about sanding Blister's horns and applying oil to make them shine.

At the back end hangs Blister's tail, an extremity which requires a particularly deft touch. Since you are the deft touch expert of the family, this job is assigned to you. First, clip the tail from its root end to just above the fluffy part called "the switch". Start at the base of the tail. WARNING: The tail of a bull hangs limply downward. However, it can suddenly whip up, around and back and forth like an aggressive snake, to flail face and body. Should the tail chance to be untidy, you may receive more than a lashing. Therefore, it is best to tie the tip of the appendage to one of the bull's legs. (A back one, of course.) Clip carefully downwards, all around, to just above the switch. Then fill a bucket with warm soapy water and dip Blister's tail into it. (The warm water is for your benefit, not the bull's.) Slip on those big black or orange, rubber work gloves, pick up a stiff scrub brush and proceed to shampoo Blister's switch. Chances are, what with everything else that's taking place all over him, he won't mind you messing about with his tail. After the shampoo, brush, comb and fluff the switch.* (see footnote) Caution: while you are beautifying Blister's tail, he may from time to time, rid himself of waste material. Try not to let his freshly shampooed switch fall into any untidiness.

Finally Fair time arrives. Blister is transported along with a highly nervous son to the Fairgrounds where the calf is tied in a stall heaped with fresh clean straw. Until the moment the judges call for him, young son constantly brushes, combs, and fluffs Blister. The MOMENT arrives. You watch proudly as number one son, duded up in white western shirt AND a tie, pearl grey Stetson, brand new pants and much polished boots, leads Blister into the ring where he competes against the other entrants. Eight kids ranging in size from plumb puny to medium small, stand big-eyed before the almighty judge. The critters stand there, too, even bigger-eyed and more nervous than their young masters. The judge considers each animal carefully. How it stands, its conformation, its general bearing, its grooming and cleanliness, and how well the exhibitor manages him are all counted into the final score. Every show person in the ring is constantly combing, brushing, and scratching bellies while praying his or her animal will remain CALM. A great deal hinges on cleanliness and calmness.

At all times, the 4-H exhibitor must keep his animal between himself and the judge. Eyes glued on the judge, the kids comb and brush and scratch bellies as they set up their animals. You stand at the sidelines, fingers crossed as your son turns Blister in a tight circle. Last year his steer calf decided enough was enough and commenced to gallop toward the nearest exit dragging your offspring along at the end of the

---

* Almost always, switch grooming reminds you to make an appointment at the local people beauty emporium to have your hair done.

rope. It had proved embarrassing when you instinctively reacted by leaping in front of the departing pair. The decamping steer instantly planted his feet, spun around and knocked over the judge who had kindly come to help.

But this year all goes well. When the winners are announced and your son walks away with a blue or possibly even a purple "best of show" ribbon, you have to slip under the grandstand for a second, because for some foolish reason your eyes are watering.

The hard work preparing the animal, the labor of special record keeping, feeds used, pounds gained and rates of gain, have all been faithfully attended to by your son. Now the beautiful calf that has been so lovingly cared for must be sold. The last night of the Fair is auction sale night. Beef, pork, sheep, rabbits, chickens, vegetables—all are auctioned off to the highest bidder. Usually local business men buy the meat animals at premium prices. For your son, the trauma of parting with Blister is not as severe as for some kids. Blister is sold as breeding stock, so at least he won't be slaughtered.

After the sale, number one son's bank account swells by several hundred dollars. Already he is planning for next year when he says he's going to enter a different animal in each class. You, for one, can hardly wait.

In addition to the various stock exhibits, horsemanship competitions attract every juvenile in the county who owns a riding animal. Judging is based on performance of both horse and rider. Even little kids can enter the horsemanship event. Children under seven manage the reins of their horses, but MOTHER provides guidance by leading the pony with a halter rope. Mother leads the mount at a walk and then at a trot while the judge observes the child's horsemanship ability. No loping is required in this event. The horse and the child are willing. It's Mother who limits the action. Some pudgy mothers can barely manage to trot alongside a steed, let alone gallop.

However, the competition is keen. All the kids, ponies, horses, and mothers appear clad in assorted eye-appealing garb. At least most do. According to the rules the judge makes his choice on the basis of horsemanship and ability. It says so in the rule book. WARNING: Beware of false belief in the printed word.

At the fairgrounds, watch proudly as number two son, age four and a half, mounts his noble steed by pulling himself up hand over hand on the stirrup leathers. Dressed in his brand new denim pants, his almost new straw cowboy hat, red checkered shirt, and lovingly polished boots, young son shines among all the others. How could a judge fail to be impressed with so obviously smart and handsome a child seated royally astride his recently cleaned saddle on his very own fat, brown, half Welsh pony?

Overwhelmed with pride, distract yourself by peering misty-eyed around the grounds at the less fortunate mothers. Suddenly you notice Mrs. Super Rancher leading a prancing, slim, high-headed sorrel mare. A silver bedecked saddle glints, hurting your eyes. Fancy pink tassels dangle from the bridle. A matching pink leather halter and pink lead rope complete the horse's wardrobe. You consider the plain rope halter leading to your son's pony, a much more practical choice. Then your lip freezes into a permanent curl as you note Mrs. Super Rancher's five year old daughter, Melanie Ann. The dear little thing wears an ensemble of pink topped with a pink western hat trimmed with a silver band. White western boots match the white kid gloves encasing the tot's dainty hands. All that pink is about to give you an eye disease. Particularly as Mrs. Super Rancher wears a pink outfit that exactly matches her daughter's! You are dressed less ostentatiously in serviceable, but clean denim jeans and plain unadorned western shirt. (Some people have more restrained taste in clothes than others.)

Naturally, as the judge calls for the participants, you and son are placed in line directly behind Mrs. Super Rancher and Melanie Ann. Take a deep breath and straighten yourself until you feel thin. Remember to exhale, too, so you don't black out. Take heart from your son who sits tall in the saddle. His pony thinks the whole thing is a bore and tries to grab a mouthful of grass, jerking you off your brave stance.

But you can't let your son down, so lift up your chin and stride briskly forth in an attempt to wake up the pony. Smile as you walk and trot past the judges. On the far side of the arena, bring the pony to a halt. You are supposed to demonstrate the horse's backing ability. Whisper to your son to use the kleenex you sneakily hand him. Then carry on. Young son is thrilled with everything. Preening, he waves grandly to his friends in the audience. At that moment, his pony decides to shake off his depression and does so with a head to tail quiver that rattles the saddle and the boy. Turning back from his waving, number two son gruffly reprimands his mount with a loud, "Cut that out, you old crowbait!" His four and a half year old voice cuts across the crowd, clear as a bell. The pony, taking the command as a cue to move forward, does so and treads onto your foot. Your quick acting son pulls the critter to a halt while he is still on your foot. Try not to allow tears to form. It interferes with vision and makes you seem unsportsmanlike.

When the ribbons are awarded, a blue one goes to Melanie Ann Super Rancher on her horse, "Little Misty's Golden Princess". Second and third place go to a couple of kids other than your child. Your son, on his fat pony, "Skeezik's Lament", rides proudly forward along with the remaining field of sixteen kids who each receive a plain white ribbon for "showmanship".

By this time your stomach muscles have gone slack. Concentrate everything on the pleasant smile you bestow upon Mrs. Super Rancher. Congratulate Melanie Ann and try not to lose the smile as Mrs. Super Rancher mentions what a "terribly cute little outfit" your son is wearing.

SECTION THIRTY-SEVEN: BASIC RANCH ATTITUDES
(A Ranch is a Ranch is a Ranch. . .)

Wherein one learns that regardless of the labor, the chapped and peeling complexion, the lack of elegance, and the dearth of shopping centers, one still counts oneself the luckiest person in the world.

No country woman has to worry or wonder about her "role". It's a partnership arrangement. You, your husband and the kids work continuously to wrest from nature a decent living. As a country woman, you are sure of one important thing. You share the battle. You share good and bad. You share the terrific feeling when the ranch has a good year. You share the thrill the time there's almost a hundred per cent live calf crop. You also share the gloom the year the grasshoppers eat the corn and hail ruins the wheat just before harvest. One winter you share all the feeding chores with the kids when your husband has a fractured leg. If there's one thing a Ranch Woman is not, it's pampered. But it's an exultant feeling to know you're a part of every aspect of the business of living. As a Country Woman you know how many critters are due to calve, or lamb, or pig. You know when the haying is due to start, when the cattle have to be rounded up, and what to expect from the livestock buyers. Every member of the family is an important and responsible part of the operation.

Unlike the city woman who associates with her spouse only during weekends and on social occasions, you live every day all day with your man. There's no such thing as keeping business and home life separate on a ranch!

And there's lots of room in the country. There's room for the Ranch Woman to have plenty of daily opportunity to admire her Ranch Man. By the time the city man goes to work at eight or nine, your man has put in half a day's hard physical work before breakfast. He's a loveable character with a limitless capacity for hard labor. Soft spoken (except in the corrals under certain circumstances), he quietly manages all the toughest jobs around the place. He can ride, lift all that heavy stuff, drive machinery, deliver calves, throw bales, shear sheep, rope critters, shoe horses, make speeches at the local farmer's meetings, get involved with farm and ranch politics if necessary, figure the best nutritional balance for feeding livestock, do carpentering and electrical work, doctor animals, build corrals, and tote his kids patiently around with him teaching them from his own experiences.

There's a poetry and a soul filling satisfaction for those who like working with land and animals. Some city folks are misplaced farmers at heart and would take to country life like the proverbial ducks to water. However, a working farm or ranch is not for the idealistic dreamer who depends on "magic thinking." Magic thinkers tend to be unable to relate the application of the shovel to the ditch or the manure pile. They feel nature and God will manage everything. Through mystical contemplation alone, the animals and the crops and the gardens will produce, and the glorious bounty will fall into the Magic Thinkers' open mouths. With all due respect to the Deity, nature and contemplation, crops, animals and gardens sure do better if you help! Ranchers and farmers face a constant backbreaking, fiercely competitive fight against the weather, floods, drought, disease, and predators, followed closely by taxes and governmental regulations. The battle rages each year and each year it is never really won—at best it's a standoff.

However, be it a good year or a poor one, if you're lucky enough to live in the country, you're guaranteed to have one heck of a good time! There's nowhere else you'd rather be. Wherever you go, whatever you do on the ranch or the farm— toting a snack to the hay fields, trotting out to the corrals or the milk barn, saddling up the mare for the roundup, collecting the eggs, picking berries along the creek banks—you sure know you're alive and living in the country. The miracle of every day's small incidents and routine happenings constantly help you reckon you're a Country Woman.

For example you know you live on a ranch or farm:

   ... when the increasing height and breadth of the manure pile gives you a warm feeling of pride.

... when you glance out the window to note your man marching up the path, a newborn, half-dead calf dangling over his shoulder, and you automatically jump to spread a blanket behind the stove.

... when eating storebought bread is a treat.

... when other women brag about their household achievements and you brag about the three sets of triplet lambs.

... when your youngest son in kindergarten describes the birth of a calf during "show and tell" starting with, "First, a big bubble comes out the back . . ."

... when you laugh wildly because town women call you to serve on assorted projects because "you don't work."

... when a city kid comes to visit and you overhear number one son explaining the function of the little house out back with the two-holer seat.

... when King, the 70 pound collie, hits a skunk, sneaks in the house and jumps on the bed.

... when your husband sleeps on the couch all during Columbo, his favorite program.

... when you open the refrigerator door and a vaccine bottle drops into the jello.

... when your man pleads with you to drop everything and drive immediately to town. It's an emergency— he's out of Snoose.

... when it's five minutes before supper and you're scraping the leftover peas into the leftover potatoes, planning for soup and crackers. Just then you hear your rancher man on the back stoop cheerfully assuring a whole gaggle of extra men, "Sure, there's plenty! C'mon in!"

... when you wash your face, put on lipstick, and a fresh blouse, and your husband wants to know where you're going "all gussied up."

... when "dinner" means a ten course meal served precisely at high noon.

... when everyone you know or ever did know thinks a perfect vacation is a visit to a ranch—yours.

. . . when Peek-a-Boo, the pet sow, roots open the back door to the utility room, finds a full milk bucket and a basket of laundry and proceeds to blend everything into porridge.

. . . when Lancelot, the banty rooster, likes to perch on your head and crow.

. . . when your hands and arms swell up for a week from picking buffalo berries.

. . . when you try to educate a city friend in the art of butchering her own chickens so as to economize and she turns green and leaves the room in the middle of your recital.

. . . when you accidentally inject yourself while vaccinating the cows and have to go see the Vet instead of the MD.

. . . when you get drafted to milk the heifer milk cow who has just come fresh and your hands swell up like sausages.

. . . when your heart lurches, just like in books, at the breath-taking crystal beauty of the mountains against the spring sky.

. . . when you see the row of gray fence posts marching, in measured formation across the winter snow.

. . . when the miracle of new grass in spring begins to push green threads among the winter brown and gray.

. . . when your favorite sow has fourteen nice healthy piglets and she loves them all.

. . . when the hot summer nurtures each moment of the day in a cocoon of peace.

. . . when a wintertime chinook makes you feel as bouncy as a calf.

And you really know you're a Ranch or Farm Woman when your man puts his arm around you as you both lean over the corral fence watching the fat hogs eat up that expensive grain, and he declares, "Happy Anniversary, you Old Heifer!"